Flights of Fancy

Peter Tate has published several books on ornithology, including *Bird, Men and Books: A Literary History of Ornithology* and *A Century of Bird Books*. When his publisher Anthony Witherby passed away, he placed the manuscript of his next book quietly away on a shelf and there it remained until it was rediscovered several years later.

Praise for *Flights of Fancy*

'Here is a book that will change the way we look at our feathered friends for ever.' *National Trust Magazine*

'Some of the rituals constructed around birds are truly extraordinary, as Peter Tate's exquisitely produced book reveals . . . there are wondrous tales from all over the globe here.' *Financial Times*

'Well-known ornithologist Tate moves on from just observing birds to bring us wonderful stories and historical anecdotes.' *Good Book Guide*

'The author has used a lifetime of accumulating stories and distilled that knowledge into a very readable and entertaining summary . . . I would recommend this book as an enjoyable read.' *London Naturalist*

'Peter Tate here presents a rich fund of traditional beliefs.' *Ibis*

'Fascinating and entertaining, this book is a fun read for anyone who's interested in

'This is a qu   but gorgeously

'*Flights of F   and should remain) nature   *Times Literary Supplement*

Flights of Fancy

Birds in Myth, Legend
and Superstition

PETER TATE

arrow books

Published by Arrow Books 2009

2 4 6 8 10 9 7 5 3 1

Copyright © Peter Tate 2007

Peter Tate has asserted his right under the Copyright, Designs
and Patents Act 1988 to be identified as the author of this work

First published in Great Britain in 2007 by
Random House Books
Random House, 20 Vauxhall Bridge Road,
London SW1V 2SA

www.rbooks.co.uk

Addresses for companies within The Random House Group Limited can be found at:
www.randomhouse.co.uk/offices.htm

The Random House Group Limited Reg. No. 954009

A CIP catalogue record for this book
is available from the British Library

ISBN 9780099509875

The Random House Group Limited supports The Forest Stewardship
Council (FSC), the leading international forest certification organisation. All our
titles that are printed on Greenpeace approved FSC certified paper carry the FSC logo.
Our paper procurement policy can be found at www.rbooks.co.uk/environment

Design by Dinah Drazin

Printed and bound in Great Britain by
CPI Cox & Wyman, Reading, RG1 8EX

For Anne

Contents

Introduction   ix

Blackbird   1
Cockerel   4
Crane   11
Crossbill   19
Cuckoo   22
Diver   30
Dove   35
Eagle   41
Goose   50
Hoopoe   58
House sparrow   64
Kingfisher   67
Lapwing   72
Magpie   76
Nightingale   81
Nightjar   88
Owl   91
Peacock   99
Pelican   103

Quail	106
Raven	111
Robin	118
Rook	125
Stonechat	128
Stork	130
Swallow	133
Swan	142
Woodpecker	149
Wren	154
Wryneck	160
Authors quoted or mentioned in the text	163
Gods and goddesses	167
Bibliography	169
Index	171

Introduction

From the significance of the first cuckoo to rhymes about magpies, an astonishingly large and varied body of folklore has grown up around birds. Some of the stories that have been handed down through the generations are quite straightforward, such as the belief that it's bad luck to kill a robin. Others are amazingly elaborate or bizarre, such as the Greek folk-cure for a headache, which involved removing the head of a swallow at the full moon, then leaving it in a linen bag to dry. They can be found in all parts of the world, from the story of Yorimoto in Japan, who hid from his enemies in a tree and was protected by two doves, to the strange tale of Gertrude in Germany, who was turned into a woodpecker as punishment for her miserliness. What they all show is just how fascinated mankind has always been by birds. They are, after all, creatures that occupy a very particular and unusual place in our lives. On the one hand, they seem very familiar: they build nests in our gardens or in the eaves of our houses; some have even been domesticated and play an important role in agriculture to this day. On the other hand, they also inhabit a completely different realm from our own – one that we land-bound creatures can only imagine and wonder at. It seems scarcely surprising, therefore, that they should have proved such a rich source of speculation and myth-making.

What I have tried to do in this book is not to attempt an exhaustive survey of traditional beliefs about birds – such a survey would take up many hundreds of pages – but to select the stories that have most intrigued me in the course of a lifetime's study. For example, I knew that migration was not fully understood before the eighteenth century, but I was fascinated to discover that many people used to believe that cuckoos turned into hawks when they departed for the winter months. I'm also intrigued by stories that recur in different traditions. The belief that birds with black plumage, such as crows and ravens, originally had white feathers but were punished for some crime or other, for example, is very widely spread. Similarly, tales of swan maidens can be found as far afield as India, Greenland and Ireland. Perhaps the strangest example of a well-travelled tale is that told of cranes. I first came across the belief that every winter migrating cranes do battle with pygmies in Aristotle's *History of Animals*. I was astonished, years later, to come across precisely the same story among the Cherokees of the south-eastern USA. I still have no idea how the same story came to be told in places so many thousands of miles apart.

Of course, many of the stories recorded here were almost certainly told just for fun originally. Some, no doubt, were old wives' tales, told to scare or instruct youngsters. Some reflect people's desperate desire to control the present or foretell the future through natural signs – such as the belief in Snowdonia that circling eagles portended victory on the battlefield. One story, however, can lay good claim to having a place – or at least a footnote – in history. It concerns the barnacle goose, which in medieval times was variously described as a bird or, thanks to some rather confused travellers' tales, as a sort of fish that hatched from barnacles. Since Catholic countries had strict rules on what could be eaten when, the barnacle goose debate was eventually picked up by the Church, and in 1215 one of the most powerful of all medieval popes, Innocent III, felt compelled to weigh in and make a judgement on the matter at the Fourth Lateran Council. It's a nice reminder of how central to people's lives story-making can be.

My thanks go to my agent Charlotte Vamos, without whom this book would never have taken flight. I would also like to thank the editorial team at Random House: Nigel Wilcockson, Caroline Pretty and Sophie Lazar.

Blackbird
(Turdus merula)

A rather plump species of thrush with very obvious differences between males and females. The male blackbird lives up to its name and has black feathers with a bright orange bill, while the female is mainly dark brown. One of Northern Europe's most familiar birds, it can be found in most gardens and parks. Its song is clear, beautiful and distinctive, making blackbirds one of the most recognizable songsters.

Like so many birds with a black plumage, blackbirds were once thought to have been white. In Brescia in Italy, for example, it was believed that the blackbird changed colour as a result of a cruel and cold winter. Forced to take shelter from the wind and snow, the bird sought refuge in a chimney, where it became blackened by the soot. In commemoration, the last two days of January and the first of February became known as *i giorni della merla*, 'the blackbird days'. White blackbirds can also be found in ancient Greek tradition: Aristotle describes them in his *History of Animals* as living on Mount Cyllene in Arcadia. These mythical birds were supposed to have a wider range of notes than other blackbirds and to appear only by moonlight.

An alternative legend was recorded by the nineteenth-century French author Eugene Rolland. It tells how a white blackbird, while lurking in a thicket, was greatly astonished to discover a magpie hiding diamonds, jewellery and golden coins in her nest.

Upon asking the magpie how he too might acquire such a treasure, he received the reply:

'You must seek out in the bowels of the earth the palace of the Prince of Riches, offer him your services and he will allow you to carry off as much treasure as you can carry in your beak. You will have to pass through many caverns each more overflowing with riches than the last, but you must particularly remember not to touch a single thing until you have actually seen the Prince himself.'

The blackbird immediately went to the entrance of the subterranean passage to discover the treasure. The first cavern he had to pass through was lined with silver, but he managed to keep the magpie's advice in mind and continue on his way. The second cavern was ablaze with gold, and though the blackbird

tried to master himself, it proved too much for him and he plunged his beak into the glittering dust with which the floor was strewn. Rolland continues:

> Immediately there appeared a terrible demon vomiting fire and smoke who rushed up to the wretched bird with such lightning speed that the bird escaped with the greatest difficulty. But alas the thick smoke had besmirched forever his white plumage and he became as now, quite black with the exception of his bill which still preserves the colour of the gold he was so anxious to carry off.

This legend also sought to account for the piercing cries of terror uttered by a blackbird when startled: it claims the bird is expecting to be attacked by another terrible demon.

Blackbirds tend not to play much of a part in religious stories (unlike, for example, doves and ravens), and where they do appear their role is generally a subsidiary one. One rather charming story tells of St Kevin (498–618), an Irish saint who, like St Francis of Assisi, preferred the company of animals to humans and was said to have a mystical command over them. Once, when he was praying during Lent, a blackbird landed on his outstretched hand and laid an egg there. St Kevin then remained perfectly still until the egg had hatched – an illustration of the virtuous saint's patience and gentleness.

Although the blackbird is not generally credited with the gift of prophecy, there is a reference to its weather-forecasting ability in a saying from County Meath in Ireland: 'When the blackbird sings before Christmas, she will cry before

Candlemas'. This means that if the bird should start to sing before its usual time of early to mid February, a cold spell will occur before 2 February, when the rite of Candlemas is observed. Blackbirds were also the subject of weather-based superstitions in Germany, where it was thought that a blackbird kept caged in a house offered protection against lightning.

Cockerel
(Gallus gallus)

Bred from oriental junglefowl which originated in India, Burma and South-East Asia. Over the years, selective breeding has vastly altered its form and colours, ranging from white to black with many variations in-between. Known as roosters in North America and Australia, the female of the species is the hen.

As urban society has spread and farming practices have changed, the waking of the whole community by a farmyard cockerel who crows at first light has all but ceased to exist. But not so long ago, when country dwellers had no watches or clocks, the farm worker's day literally began at cockcrow. This use of cockerels as alarm clocks seems to have been universal in countries where they had been domesticated. In Abyssinia, for example, the Coptic Church used cockerels to rouse local villagers to worship.

Cockerels are associated with many different aspects of folk-lore, from augury to popular legend, and many of the ideas

4

and stories about them go back to very early times. In Greece, for example, where the bird was first introduced in around 700 BC, it became linked with several of the gods: it was dedicated to Apollo, the sun god, as people believed that its crowing heralded the sunrise and its red comb symbolized the sun; it was also sacred to Hermes, the winged messenger; and it was associated with Ares, the god of war, perhaps because of its reputation for vigilance and valour (one was even reputed to have put a lion to flight).

One story about Ares and a cockerel, however, casts the cockerel in a less flattering light. It tells how Ares planned to spend the night with Aphrodite, the goddess of love, and ordered a cockerel to keep watch for Aphrodite's husband, Hephaestus (the blacksmith god). Unfortunately, the bird fell asleep, and when Hephaestus came home unexpectedly he caught the couple together. Deciding to embarrass rather than punish them, Hephaestus bound them to the couch on which they lay and called the other gods to come and see how ridiculous they looked.

Perhaps because they have been so closely associated with vigilance, cockerels are often linked to augury and divination. The Greeks invented a method of forecasting in which grains of corn marked with letters of the alphabet were fed to cockerels. The order in which the birds pecked at them was carefully noted and used to make predictions. A more simplified version of this method was recorded in Roman times: unmarked grain was fed to a group of hens, known as sacred chickens, and if they fed so eagerly that some spilt from their beaks it was considered a good omen. So important were the predictions of sacred chickens that the Roman army carried a cage of the birds with it wherever it went, and even appointed an official sacred-chicken keeper, known as the pullarius.

In *De Natura Deorum* (*On the Nature of the Gods*), Cicero tells a salutary tale about the great Roman general Publius Claudius (d. 249/246 BC), who foolishly disregarded the importance of these sacred birds:

> Shall we remain unimpressed by the tale of the presumptuous conduct of Publius Claudius in the first Punic war, who, when the sacred chickens, on being let out of the coop, refused to

feed, ordered them to be plunged into the water, that they might, as he said, drink, since they would not eat? He only ridiculed the gods in jest, but the mockery cost him many a tear (for his fleet was utterly routed), and brought a great disaster upon the Roman people.

Central and North European pagan beliefs link the cockerel with both the corn god and fertility. In Britain, the cockerel not only formed part of the harvest celebrations, but was also used in a number of the fertility ceremonies that took place at the time of the sowing of the crops. These tended to cluster around Shrove Tuesday and generally involved some sort of sacrifice. One example was 'Cockshies', when a cockerel was tied to a pole so that men could throw stones at it, rather like at a coconut shy. Whoever killed the bird was allowed to keep the carcass. The same rite was practised in France, while in Transylvania the cockerel would be cut up and mixed with the seed corn destined for the following year's harvest. An even crueller ritual was one where a cockerel was buried in the ground with only its head protruding. As the harvesters cut the last stalks of corn, the cockerel's head would be cut off.

As well as being linked with the harvest, the cockerel was also closely associated with medicine and healing, often being employed in rather bizarre rituals. For example, in Transylvania when a woman left her house for the first time after having a baby, a cockerel (or a hen, if the newborn child was a girl) would be cut in half and the two sections nailed to the doorpost. The idea was that magic properties from the bird would pass to the new mother and help her to regain her health and strength.

Bird stones

Many different species of birds were thought to carry stones with magical properties. Here are just a few:

- The Romans believed that cockerels could hide a stone known as *alectorius* in their gizzards. If you were lucky enough to find one, it had the power to make you invisible.
- Eagle stones were thought to be hollow and red or black with yellow spots. They contained a second stone that rattled about inside them. Found in the birds' nests, they were much prized as an aid to childbirth.
- Hoopoe stones could force confessions from sleeping men.
- It was believed that there were three different types of raven stone: the release stone, which was used to aid childbirth; the invisibility stone, which when clasped under the right armpit would make you disappear; and the life stone, which was the most valuable of all.
- The skulls of storks were thought to contain a stone that could be used as an antidote to poison.
- Swallows were thought to carry two different stones with them. One was red and could cure an invalid instantly, the other was black and brought good fortune.

The beneficial properties of the cockerel were noted by the Roman writer and naturalist Pliny the Elder. He suggested that stewing and eating red cockerel would provide protection against wild beasts and also grant extra strength. In a similar fashion, during the Middle Ages, a brew called 'Cock Ale', prepared from a boiled red cockerel and strong ale, was thought to make people stronger.

Many ancient pagan beliefs and customs were adopted and then adapted by Christians, often resulting in a strange amalgam of Christian and pagan rites. A good example of just such a meeting of cultures could once be found at Llandegla in Wales, where a well near the church was thought to have magic properties. Sufferers from 'falling sickness' (epilepsy) would bathe in the well, then walk round it three times while reciting the Lord's prayer, before throwing in some money. Following this, a cockerel or a hen (depending on the sex of the sufferer) would be carried ceremoniously round the church and the well. Finally, the patient would take the bird and spend the night lying beneath the altar. At the end of the night, it was thought that the sickness would be transferred to the bird, and as recently as 1850 an onlooker reported that he had seen birds 'staggering about' after the ritual.

Another belief that certainly persisted until the nineteenth century was that to bury a cockerel under a church, or indeed any building, was a guaranteed way to ward off evil. But of course the cockerel's main connection with Christianity comes from the New Testament account of Jesus's crucifixion. The Gospel writers record that at the Last Supper, Jesus predicted that his closest disciple, Peter, would deny him three times before cockcrow. Peter duly did so, and, on the third occasion, as Luke records:

> And the Lord turned, and looked upon Peter. And Peter remembered the word of the Lord, how he had said unto him, Before the cock crow, thou shalt deny me thrice.
>
> And Peter went out, and wept bitterly.

The weathervanes that can often be found on church towers and spires were traditionally made in the form of a cockerel to serve as a reminder to all believers that they must not deny their God.

The cockerel plays a significant role in traditional Islamic tales about Muhammad's *mir'aj*, his travels through the seven heavens. It was said that he met a huge cockerel during his journey whose duty it was to wake every living creature with the exception of man. Muhammad was told that when this cockerel ceased to crow, the world would come to an end. There is an Arab saying that Allah will always listen to those who pray for pardon, to those who read the Koran, and to the cockerel, whose chant is divine melody.

The flood legend, inextricably linked for many in Judaeo-Christian cultures to the story of Noah and his ark, exists in various guises all over the world, and in Upper Burma the Singpho people tell a version in which cockerels play an important part. When the deluge came, a man named Pawpaw Nanchaung and his sister Chang-hko saved themselves by building a large boat. They took with them nine cockerels and nine needles, which they threw overboard day after day to see if the waters had abated. On the ninth day, the cockerel was heard to crow and the needle was heard to hit the bottom, and so Pawpaw Nan-chaung and Chang-hko knew they would be able to find dry land.

Two rather strange beliefs used to exist in Scotland. One of these said that if a cockerel reached the age of thirteen it would lay an egg from which would hatch a cockatrice, a mythical creature which breathed fire and could cause harm merely by its glance. Cockatrices, also known as basilisks, feature in many medieval bestiaries, and it was frequently recorded that the weasel was the only animal that could harm them. The other Scottish belief was that if a cockerel crowed during the night, the owner should at once get up and feel the bird's feet. If they felt cold, a death would soon occur, but if they were warm then good news was on the way. In both the West Country and Essex it was thought that should a cockerel crow at midnight, then the angel of death was flying over the house and death would soon come to someone inside it.

Crane
(Grus grus)

A very large and graceful long-legged bird, standing almost a metre high. It is migratory, and is capable of travelling long distances between Northern Europe and Africa. Nests in mainly marshy areas, eating crops, insects, snails and worms. Primarily grey in colour.

In Europe, where it is a summer visitor that breeds mainly in the north of the continent, the crane is best known as a spectacular migrant; indeed, anyone who has seen or heard a flock of cranes flying in their great 'V' shaped formations is unlikely to forget the experience.

Not surprisingly, past generations were fascinated by these huge migrating flocks, and a considerable body of myths and legends grew up around them. The most widely held belief was that cranes frequently carried small birds on their backs during the long migratory flights, especially when crossing over water. The German traveller Ebeling, writing in 1878, related how he had been told by some Egyptians that yellow wagtails and other small birds waited for the cranes to arrive and then perched on their backs for the sea crossing. The same belief was held by Bedouin tribesmen, who also claimed that the reason why the cranes were prepared to carry these little birds on their journeys was because they enjoyed their singing.

The Crow Indians of Montana believe that sandhill cranes carry a small bird which they call the 'napite-shu-utl' or 'cranes-back'. In a similar vein, the Arawak Indians of Venezuela believe that the all-important tobacco plant was brought to their ancestors by a thieving hummingbird who stole it from Trinidad and then hitched a ride on a crane to South America.

In 1740, the German naturalist Johann Georg Gmelin was assured by Tartars that all the corncrakes in Siberia were carried to the south on the backs of cranes and storks, while in 1919 Mr Hagland of Therien in Alberta wrote to the American naturalist Ernest Ingersoll:

One fall a flock of cranes passed over me flying very low and apart from their squawking I could distinctly hear the twittering of small birds, sparrows of some kind. The chirping grew louder as the cranes drew towards me, and grew fainter as they drew away and as the cranes were the only birds in sight I concluded that little birds were taking a free ride to the south.

Eyewitness ornithological records should never be dismissed lightly, but it seems in this case that Mr Hagland made an honest mistake. His inaccurate observation, however, serves to show how such a widespread belief could have arisen in the first place. In reality, it is highly improbable that a small bird would be able, or indeed permitted, to travel on a flying crane. That said, there is certainly one example known of a large bird carrying a smaller one – though only on the ground. The kori bustard of Southern Africa sometimes allows carmine bee-eaters to ride on its back while it stalks through the grass. As the larger bird stirs up the insects, the bee-eaters catch them.

Cranes have attracted other myths, too. One, mentioned by Pliny the Elder in the first century BC, is that at the start of their annual migrations they swallowed stones, using them as ballast in order to avoid being swept off course by changing winds. Their journey completed, the cranes would vomit up the stones, which would then serve as valuable touchstones, allowing the finder to identify gold-bearing rocks. Cranes were also said by some to use stones as a form of warning device. While resting between migratory flights, the birds would post sentries to watch for surprise attacks, and these lookout birds would stand on one leg and carry a stone in the other. Should they happen to doze off, their grip on the stone would loosen and it would fall to the ground, waking them up in the process. In heraldic devices representing vigilance, cranes are often depicted standing on one leg, holding a stone in the other.

There are also fables that tell of cranes' relationships with humans. One such tale originates from north-western Alaska and seeks to explain why cranes circle round, calling continuously before they depart for the south. One autumn day, the tale goes, the birds saw an Inuit girl standing alone near a village. She was so beautiful that they encircled her, lifted her aloft on their wings and carried her away. Meanwhile, others flew in a dense flock below ready to catch her if she fell, calling loudly in order to drown the sound of her screams. According to the Inuit, cranes still behave in this manner before setting off on their migration because they want to find a beautiful woman to take with them.

One question that seems to have been a constant cause of fascination was: what did cranes do once they arrived in the south? The Greeks thought that, during the winter, cranes engaged in battle with pygmies. In his *History of Animals*, Aristotle informs us that:

> ... these birds migrate from the steppes of Scythia to the marshlands south of Egypt where the Nile has its source. And it is here, by the way, that they are said to fight with the pygmies; and the story is not fabulous, but there is in reality a race of dwarfish men, and the horses are little in proportion, and the men live in caves underground ...

This seems an astonishingly bizarre idea. Almost as extraordinary is the fact that the Greeks were not alone in believing it. For example, a Chinese text, the Shen ī king, written in the fourth or fifth century states:

In the region of the Sihai (the Mediterranean) is the land of the cranes (hao kuo) where men and women are only seven inches tall. The only creatures they fear are cranes which come here from the sea. The cranes which in one single flight travel a thousand miles can gobble them (the pygmies) up.

Similarly, the fourteenth-century Egyptian scholar Musa ud Damiri in his *Hayat al-Hayawan* (*The Life of Animals*) describes battles between little people and large birds – and though the birds here are said to be storks, the story in other respects belongs to the traditions concerning cranes. In Musa ud Damiri's version of events, some storm-driven travellers came to an island where the inhabitants were about three feet tall and only had one eye. Shortly afterwards a flock of storks came and attacked the pygmies by pecking at their single eye.

The fact that stories of large birds attacking pygmies were known in countries as far apart as Greece, Egypt and China can probably be explained in terms of the trading links that existed from very early times. But it's hard to explain why remarkably similar myths could also exist among some of the North American Indian tribes.

The Cherokees, for example, whose ancestral home was in the south-east of the USA, have a legend which tells of a journey by some young men of the tribe who wished to see the world. They travelled south until they came upon a tribe of very little people, the Tsundige'wi, who had strangely shaped bodies and who barely reached up to a man's knee. These little men lived in nests in the sand that were covered with dry grass, and they were terrified of the wild geese that came in great flocks from the south and attacked them. When the Cherokees arrived, the Tsundige'wi were in a state of great anxiety, because the wind was blowing from the south, bringing with it some white feathers, and this was a sure sign that the birds were not far away. The Cherokees asked why they did not defend themselves against the birds, but the dwarfs said they had no weapons. The Cherokees did not have time to make bows and arrows for them, but they did show them how to use sticks as clubs so that they could hit the birds on their necks and kill them. The birds flew in from the south in great flocks and the little men ran to their nests to hide. But when the birds stuck their long beaks into the nests and began to pull the men out to eat them, the men dashed out with their clubs and hit the birds as the Cherokees had shown them. They killed so many that after a while the birds flew away. For some time the Tsundige'wi were able to keep the birds at bay, until eventually a flock of sandhill cranes arrived. These birds were much taller, and the little men weren't able to strike them on the neck, and so, unfortunately for the Tsundige'wi, they all perished.

At least three other North American tribes have legends about a small race being attacked by birds, but the species are not identified. It is difficult to understand how pygmies came to feature at all in American legends as we have no hard evidence that they have ever lived on the continent. We do have folk references, however, in the form of many drawings of potbellied pygmies in the art of the Olmecs, a pre-Columbian tribe who lived in southern Veracruz, and numerous mentions of dwarfs in the mythology of Central American Indians.

Whether or not there is any direct connection between the

crane and pygmy myth from the eastern Mediterranean and
China and similar stories in America is impossible to ascertain.
There is still no known cultural link between these places, and
conjectured connections via some Siberian peoples remain tanta-
lizingly unproven. The only other alternative is the somewhat
unlikely assertion that the two myths arose independently.

As well as inspiring mythical tales of fights with pygmies,
cranes were also enormously popular in folk medicine. In his
long account of birds, the English naturalist Edward Topsell
(1572–1625) lists many cures that rely on parts of a crane, as
well as many recipes for cooking the bird, which was a highly
esteemed food. Their flesh was considered to be an excellent
remedy for 'Cancers, ulcers, palsy and wynde in the gutts'. He
went on to claim that broth made from a crane:

> Cleareth the voice and encreaseth the seede naturall. Arnoldus
> [a Roman authority on medicine] maketh a powder by dryinge
> their head, eyes, belly, ribbes and gutts for the cure of fistulas,
> ulcers and cancers. Pliny saieth that the nerves taken out of
> their leggs or wings doe helpe a wearied man to recover strength
> and beinge applied to laborers keepe them from wearysomnes.
> The fatt which swymmeth when the crane is in seethinge
> [boiling], if it bee taken of and instilled into the eares helpeth
> the deafenes and hardnes of hearinge.

The Roman naturalist Pliny the Elder wrote that the fat of
cranes 'mollified' hard swellings and other tumours, while the
Roman biographer Aelian believed that the brains of cranes
possessed aphrodisiac properties.

Crossbill
(Loxia curvirostra)

Large, heavily built member of the finch family. Most obvious feature is its massive bill with crossed mandibles. Found almost exclusively in coniferous forests in Northern Europe and North America, where it eats the seeds of fir cones which it levers open with its specially adapted bill. The males are pinkish-red, while the females and juveniles are mainly olive-coloured.

Because of their extraordinary bills, their potential to be tamed and their rarity, crossbills have long fascinated mankind and have been the focus of many different myths and legends. And whereas most other birds have attracted both praise and criticism, the crossbill has been regarded as almost entirely beneficent – even holy – with few, if any, flaws to its character.

In Thuringia in central Germany, where the crossbill was frequently kept as a caged bird, it was called the Christbird or winter bird. It was a valuable and treasured commodity, and one of its many talents was to be able to obey its master's commands. Its most desirable attribute, however, was that it could attract various human maladies to itself, so leaving its owners free from their complaints. If its bill bent to the left, it would transfer colds and rheumatism from men; if the bill curved to the right then it would cure the same complaints in women. A further medicinal property ascribed to the bird was that the water left in its drinking bowl was a certain remedy for epilepsy.

Another name for the crossbill is firebird, because of the red hue of its plumage. In Central Europe, it was thought to act as a repellent to fire, and so it was widely held that a house where a crossbill was kept in a cage would never burn down or be struck by lightning (there is a similar superstition concerning BLACKBIRDS). The crossbill was also believed to take an active role in watching over its masters: until quite recently it was said to be harmful if a child fell asleep in direct moonlight, but it was also said that crossbills would watch over the children and awaken any who were in danger of drifting off.

The holy image of the bird arose from a crucifixion legend. Prior to that day, it was held, crossbills had perfectly straight bills, but as Jesus hung above Golgotha, a crossbill swooped down and tried to help him by removing the nails. During this vain attempt, the crossbill's beak became twisted and its breast stained with Jesus's blood, hence its red plumage. The American poet and linguist Henry Wadsworth Longfellow took up this myth in his poem 'The Legend of the Crossbill', a translation from the German of Julius Mosen:

> On the cross the dying Saviour
> Heavenward lifts his eyelids calm,
> Feels, but scarcely feels, a trembling
> In his pierced and bleeding palm.

> And by all the world forsaken,
> Sees he how with zealous care
> At the ruthless nail of iron
> A little bird is striving there.

> Stained with blood and never tiring,
> With its beak it doth not cease,
> From the cross 'twould free the Saviour,
> Its Creator's Son release.

> And the Saviour speaks in mildness;
> Blest be thou of all the good!
> Bear, as token to this moment,
> Marks of blood and holy rood!

> And that bird is called the crossbill:
> Covered all with blood so clear.
> In the groves of pine it singeth
> Songs, like legends, strange to hear.

Christians found further evidence for the holiness of the crossbill in the fact that it nests very early. They believed that it laid its eggs at Christmas and that the young flew off, fully fledged, at Easter.

Cuckoo
(Cuculus canorus)

Slim and grey with a long tail and pointed wings; similar to a falcon in its general form. Distinctive two-toned call in spring. The female lays her eggs in other birds' nests so that the new parent raises a large intruder. The young cuckoo repays this hospitality by slowly pushing the other chicks out of the nest. Cuckoos migrate to Africa during the winter, an amazing journey for a bird that never meets another of its kind, having not been reared by its parents.

For countless generations, the cuckoo has been the best-known and most eagerly awaited harbinger of spring. Many of the legends concerning the time of its arrival were connected with foretelling the kind of weather to be expected during the coming summer, information of great importance for estimating the timing and magnitude of the harvest. Before people had calendars, the arrival

of the cuckoo was also an invaluable point around which to set the farming programme, as its first appearance varies by little more than a week or so from year to year.

It was widely held that the cuckoo actually brought the spring weather with it, so if it came with a fine warm spell, that sort of weather would continue. The weather was of vital importance to our ancestors, and many believed that it was decreed and sent by a deity. This deity manifested itself in many different ways all over the world, but in almost every case it needed to be appeased by offerings or sacrifices. Over the years, the regular observance of these rituals grew into the tradition of spring festivals. These would celebrate the renewal of vegetation and the return of the sun, the triumph of life over death and the hopes of a plentiful harvest to come. And the form they often took was cuckoo festivals.

There were many such festivals in Britain, and one of the last to survive was the Towednack cuckoo festival in Cornwall. This was always held on the Sunday nearest to 28 April, which itself was close to the usual date of the cuckoo's arrival. The festival was held to commemorate a legend about an old man who grew tired of waiting for winter to end. Impatient as he was, he decided to invite his friends to celebrate spring, even though it hadn't arrived yet. As he lit a large log fire for them, a cuckoo flew out of a hollow log, and was immediately followed by warm summery weather.

Perhaps because the cuckoo arrives at a time of year when many different sorts of spring festivals take place, there are quite a few amusing stories about the bird's involvement in the festivities. In Herefordshire, it was said to make a beeline for Orleton Fair on 23 April, where it would buy a horse to sell at Brompton Bruan Fair. In Worcestershire, they claimed that the bird never missed Tenbury Fair on 20 April, and was never heard after Pershore Fair on 26 June. The reason given was that the bird would buy a horse at Pershore then ride away for another year.

Traditional annual dates for the arrival of the cuckoo are different all over Europe. In the South of France, it was said that the cuckoo's song would be heard during the festival of the Feast of St Benedict (21 March). If it had not begun to sing by 25 March (Annunciation Day), then it was assumed the bird must either have been killed or have frozen to death. In Normandy it was expected to arrive on 1 April, while in parts of Germany the peasants looked for its arrival on the feast of St Valerian and St Tiburtius (14 April), the same day as the NIGHTINGALE was expected. In the north of Norway its arrival was fixed for 1 May, the feast of St Philip and St James.

By far the most elaborate of the folk ceremonies constructed around the arrival of the cuckoo took place in Pragança in Portugal. Here, a cuckoo was captured and set on a cart with two old ladies, one of whom was spinning and the other weaving. The cart would then be paraded through the streets with an escort of three hundred horsemen.

Another well-known aspect of cuckoo lore was the belief that the bird was able to help foretell the future. In Yorkshire, children used to play a game in which they danced round a cherry tree singing:

> Cuckoo, cuckoo, cherry-tree,
> Good bird, prithee, tell to me
> How many years I am to see.

Each child would then take it in turn to shake the tree, and the number of cherries which fell was said to correspond to the number of years they would live. A similar tradition existed in the west of Scotland, where it was thought that the number of calls a cuckoo made the first time it was heard predicted how many years the hearer had to live.

When unmarried women in Denmark heard a cuckoo for the first time in the year, they would kiss their hand, enquire,

'Cuckoo, cuckoo, when shall I marry?', and the number of answering calls would correspond to the number of years they would have to wait. If the cuckoo was heard to call more than ten times from different places then it was believed – fortunately, perhaps – that it must be sitting on a bewitched bough and so could be ignored.

In the west of Scotland, if listeners first heard the cuckoo before they had their breakfast, ill fortune would follow. But if they heard the bird when they had a full stomach then all would be well. Similarly, in Perigord (Dordogne) in France, if anyone first heard the cuckoo with an empty stomach it meant that the person concerned would be an idle layabout for the rest of the year or, alternatively, lose all feeling in his limbs. The only antidote to this dire predicament was to run away as fast as possible.

In Germany, to hear the cuckoo calling before a meal meant constant hunger for the next twelve months. In Denmark, if a man saw a cuckoo for the first time when he was hungry, he would be condemned not to find anything he sought. A young woman in the same situation would have to guard against being deceived by men, and old people of either sex would be subject to bad health. In Norway, for a maiden to hear the bird before breakfast was a particularly bad omen.

A widely held belief both in Britain and in continental Europe was that anyone who had money in their pockets when they first heard a cuckoo would have no need to fear poverty in the coming year. Similarly, those who heard the cuckoo's first call while in bed should prepare themselves for a death in the family.

In Northumberland, walking on a hard road when hearing the first cuckoo call presaged calamity, while being on soft ground at the time was a good omen. In Wales, it was thought that hearing the first cuckoo's call while standing on grass or something green would bring luck, while hearing it while on rocky or stony ground meant you would not live to hear the cuckoo call the following year.

Writing in the first century AD, the Roman writer and naturalist Pliny the Elder noted that when the first call of the cuckoo was heard, the soil beneath the listener's right foot acquired special magical powers so that when it was dried and sprinkled around it would kill gnats and flies. Pliny was also among those who believed that it was a bad omen for the cuckoo to call while farmers were pruning their vines. Presumably this meant that it was too late in the season for the vines to make good new growth.

A further refinement to the various myths attached to hearing the first cuckoo in spring concerned the direction from which the bird could be heard calling. In Cornwall, if the cuckoo called from the right, it signified prosperity; if from the left, ill luck. In Norway, if it should be heard calling in the north, it was a 'death cuckoo', whereas from the west it was a 'will cuckoo', signifying that the listener's wishes would be granted. A bird calling from the east ensured that the hearer's love would be returned, while a bird calling from the south foretold a good harvest.

Speculation as to when the cuckoo would arrive, where it would call from and how many times it would call was equalled by curiosity as to what became of it during the winter months. Our ancestors had no idea where it went, and many believed that it hibernated in hollow logs of wood, as already mentioned.

Some believed that when spring and summer had passed, the cuckoo changed into a bird of prey. In Cambridgeshire, it was thought that the birds were cuckoos for three months of the year before changing into hawks. Much the same belief existed in Derbyshire, with the additional twist that they sang during their transformation.

In North Germany, it was believed that cuckoos became sparrowhawks after St John's Day (24 June), whereas the Swiss felt that the birds remained cuckoos for a full year before changing. In Normandy, it was thought that the transformation took place between June and July, while other Frenchmen held that the cuckoo became a bird of prey on St James's Day (25 July) and then returned to cuckoo form in the spring, returning on the back of a kite.

Many cultures have a legend to tell about how the cuckoo used to build its own nest before it took to stealing those of others. In the border country between England and Scotland, the blame for the bird's antisocial behaviour was laid firmly on the male. He, it was said, was extremely fond of eating his own eggs and so it was in order to thwart him that the female had to hide her eggs in the nests of other birds.

In Bohemia, the tale was told that the Virgin Mary was angry with the cuckoo because it alone among the birds had continued to work on her holy day. As a punishment for this behaviour she decreed that it should be homeless for ever and never again have a nest of its own. The Danes pragmatically accounted for its nest-stealing behaviour by claiming that it was so busy answering children's questions that it hadn't the time to build a home for itself.

There is a connection between cuckoos and the word 'cuckold', which means 'husband of an unfaithful wife'. Now a rather archaic expression, the word originally meant 'adulterer', and was applied to the male bird, who was believed to seduce females of other species so that its eggs might be laid in their nests. By Shakespeare's time, the meaning had evolved, and it was the female who had come to be seen as the guilty party. The view was that she would mate with any bird in whose nest she laid her eggs, thus deceiving her partner and making him a cuckold. In the Arthurian legend, Mark, King of Cornwall, was referred to as the 'cuckold king' following his wife's love affair with Sir Tristram. And in *Love's Labour's Lost* (Act V, Scene 2), Shakespeare wrote:

> The cuckoo then on every tree
> Mocks married men, for thus sings he: Cuckoo!
> Cuckoo, cuckoo – O word of fear,
> Unpleasing to a married ear.

The Greeks were aware of the bird's breeding and nesting habits, but instead of associating the cuckoo with adultery, they linked it with lust. The cuckoo appears in one of the myriad myths concerning the amorous escapades of the gods. Theocritus tells how Zeus changed himself into a cuckoo, conjured up a great storm and then lay in wait for Hera near to Mount Thornax in Argos. When Hera saw the wet and bedraggled cuckoo, she tried to warm and dry it by putting it inside her dress. Zeus, ever the charmer, repaid her kindness by raping her.

Diver

(Gavia immer)

Sleek waterbirds with dense smooth plumage, long necks and pointed bills. They swim low in the water and dive for their food. Their legs are set very far back on the body, which means that they are extremely ungainly on land. They nearly all have wild, haunting cries.

It is often quite difficult to ascertain which myths refer to which species of diver. In the case of stories originating in the far north and North America, one can generally assume they refer to great northern or white-billed divers – known as loons – while tales from Scotland or the Faeroes (volcanic islands between Iceland and the Shetlands) are more likely to be about red-throated divers.

In many cultures, divers have been closely associated with both the beginning of the world and the end of life. Some tribes living along the Yenesei River in Siberia believed that the red-throated diver brought mud from under the waters to build the earth. The Yakuts (Turkic people from Yakutia, now part of Russia) had a similar belief, and their traditional story tells how the mother goddess sought out the white-billed diver and ordered it to collect mud to form the earth. The sneaky bird, however, tried to deceive the goddess by claiming that it could find none. Noticing that it still had mud sticking to its bill, the mother goddess uncovered the deception and condemned divers to live perpetually on the water. Other stories about the part played by the diver in making the earth are to be found all over northern Asia and North America.

Siberian shamans were fascinated by the bird's ability to dive

Soul birds

The belief that the soul migrates from the body after death is an ancient one, and a recurrent tradition in Eastern and Western mythology is that it takes temporary refuge in a bird. At sea, storm petrels and seagulls were said to house the souls of lost sailors, while shearwaters were said to carry damned souls. On land, ravens and crows were often thought to be inhabited by the souls of the dead, and there is even a tradition that King Arthur took the form of a raven when he died, as Cervantes records in his novel *Don Quixote* (1605–15):

Have you not read, sir ... the famous exploits of King Arthur ... of whom there goes an old tradition ... that this king did

beneath the surface of the water and, since they believed that the spirit world existed down there, they believed that divers could journey with humans to the other world. Wooden replicas of divers were therefore placed on tall posts at the corners of graves, and shamans not only wore ornaments in the shape of divers as part of their regalia, but also replicated their falsetto cries during the performance of rituals.

The diver was a sacred bird to the Buriats, the Yakuts and the Tungus (from western Siberia), and none of these peoples would kill or injure one. The Buriats (Mongolian people living not die, but that by magic art he was turned into a raven; and that ... he shall reign again ... for which reason it cannot be proved, that, from that time to this, any Englishman has killed a raven?

Sometimes the souls of the dead were thought to be actually carried off by birds rather than simply transferred to them. An ancient Chinese tradition held that storks carried souls up to heaven, and there is a popular story of a young man called Lan Ts'ai-ho, a talented flute-player and wandering minstrel, whose beautiful songs caused a stork to snatch him away to the heavens.

near Lake Baikal), in particular, revered the bird as they believed that the spirits of the dead would often reappear in the form of a diver. In fact, this reputation for sacredness was widespread throughout the northern reaches of the northern hemisphere. In Canada, for example, the aboriginal Algonquin tribe held that divers were the messengers of the gods. In Norway, it was thought very unwise to kill or injure a diver, and in the Faeroe Islands it was believed until the nineteenth century that divers accompanied departed souls to the next world. At Ipiutak in Alaska, ancient burial grounds have been discovered in which the graves contain skulls with ivory eyes and the skeletons of loons with similar eye plugs. It would seem that these ancient people were convinced that divers escorted and guided the dead on their last journey, rather as shamans in Siberia were later to believe.

Not only were divers thought to guide the dead, they were also believed to heal the living, and there are many tales of their restorative powers. One such tale, found in eastern Greenland, Atlantic Canada and parts of Alaska, recounts how a loon came to a blind boy and told him it had the power to make him regain his sight. It had the boy led to a lake, and there instructed him to dive in three times. The boy's sight was duly restored. The Inuit similarly believed that loons were health-giving birds, and many tribal leaders wore a loon head as a charm to endow the wearer with manly qualities. Newborn babies would be touched with a loon's skin to ensure that they would have a long and healthy life.

As well as directly aiding humans through their magical and restorative powers, divers were also thought to help humans more indirectly by forecasting the weather. The red-throated diver, which is not uncommon in Shetland, is known as the rain goose because of the noise it often makes before the arrival of bad weather. In Norway, both the black-throated and great northern divers are also credited with the ability to foretell coming storms by their calls. Strangely, the calls which the Faeroese interpret as a warning of storms are interpreted by the Shetlanders as marking the onset of fine weather.

Inevitably, given the bird's rather unusual appearance, there are a handful of legends that seek to explain why it looks the way it does. One comical explanation as to why its legs are set so far back on its body comes from Finnmark in the far north of Norway. Here it was believed that at the beginning of the world the diver was created without any legs. When the earth mother saw her mistake, she was furious at her own stupidity and threw a pair of legs after the bird. Unfortunately, they landed in the wrong place. The Norwegians also thought that the positioning of the bird's legs made it so difficult to walk that it only came ashore in the week prior to Christmas. Accordingly, they named the fourth Sunday in Advent 'Ommer Sunday', *ommer* being a corruption of *immer*, the dialect name for diver.

Dove
(Streptopelia turtur)

The turtle dove (which the ancients had in mind when writing about doves) is a delicate-looking bird, slightly bigger than a blackbird. Recently it has lost ground to the larger collared dove, introduced to Europe in the early part of the twentieth century. Unlike the migratory turtle dove, the collared dove remains in Europe.

The dove has been a symbol of peace and love since earliest recorded times. In ancient Mesopotamia, it was believed that the earth goddess, Ashtoroth, chose the dove as her emblem because of its amorous nature and fecundity. She was known by a number of different names depending on where her

devotees lived, and was called Atagartis by the Phoenicians, Astarte by the Syrians and Aphrodite by the Ionic Greeks. Wherever the Phoenicians and Levantines traded, they always erected statues to Atagartis, and every one of the statues that has been excavated features a carved dove.

Aphrodite was the goddess of love, and within that overarching title she took many different forms – some quite contradictory. On the one hand, she was Aphrodite Urania, the goddess of pure love; on the other hand, as Aphrodite Pandemas, she was the goddess of sensual, lustful and venal love and the patroness of prostitutes. The dove served as a suitable symbol for each of her attributes, being both affectionate by nature (hence the term 'lovey-dovey') and sexually very active. Interestingly, while the generally accepted story of the birth of Aphrodite is that she was produced by the foam of the sea, there is another version in which she was hatched from a dove's egg and brought ashore by a fish.

As the goddess Astarte in Syria, she had a daughter called Semiramis, who was saved from starvation in the desert by doves who fed her on milk and cheese. It was also believed that Semiramis was turned into a dove when she died.

The dove's central role in Christian lore has its roots in the Old Testament story of the dove sent out from the ark by Noah to see whether the flood that God had sent to engulf the earth had yet subsided. When the dove returned with a sprig of olive tree in its beak, Noah knew that the waters must have receded and that God had forgiven mankind. An olive branch consequently became a flag of truce or symbol of friendly intention, while the dove itself became an image of peace. In Christian iconography it also became a symbol of the Holy Ghost, shown in countless paintings and carvings hovering above the head of Jesus or the Virgin Mary or descending from the clouds in a shaft of heavenly light – a reference to the passage in St Matthew's Gospel (3: 16): 'and lo, the heavens were opened unto him, and he saw the spirit of God descending like a dove, and lighting upon him.' One apocryphal story even goes so far as to say that a dove landed on Joseph's head to show that he had been chosen as an earthly husband of Mary.

Several of the saints were said to have communicated with God through the medium of a dove which appeared at some crucial moment, alighting on either their heads or hands. The choice of Fabian as Pope in 236, for example, was believed to have been divinely confirmed when a dove landed on his shoulder. Similarly, a heavenly dove is said to have appeared at the consecration of the Merovingian French king Clovis on Christmas Day 496 in Rheims. When Bishop Remi and Clovis reached the baptistery, the priest who was carrying the chrism (the mixture of consecrated oil and balm) was cut off from them by the great crowds that had gathered to witness the event. A shining white dove bearing a vial of chrism was seen to emerge from the heavens, and so St Remi was able to perfume the baptismal water. Even though Clovis already had a reputation as a military genius, many believed that the victories he went on to win against the Germanic hordes were influenced by this heavenly intervention. Such, indeed, was the dove's reputation as a heavenly creature that it was believed in medieval times that while the Devil often visited the earth in a variety of disguises, the one form he was unable to take was that of a dove.

Throughout much of the Middle East, the dove was held to be sacred, and even today great flocks of pigeons and doves may be seen around many mosques. During the Imam Shakir Padshah's military attempt to convert the Buddhist inhabitants of Chinese Turkestan to Islam (c.119), he was killed in battle and buried in a shrine at Kaptor Massar. It is recorded that as he was being interred, two doves flew out from his heart and that these became the ancestors of the great flocks of birds which still fly around the shrine. Additionally, it was believed that if any bird of prey tried to harm the doves, it would drop dead.

A dove features in one the adventures of Jason and the Argonauts, being employed, according to Apollonius (*c.*295–215 BC), to trick the Symplegades, two islands that stood at the narrow entrance to the Straits of Bosporus and clashed together to crush any ship that tried to pass between them. Fortunately, King Phineus had given the hero wise advice about how to thwart these deadly rocks:

'First entrust the attempt to a dove when ye have sent her forth from the ship. And if she escapes safe with her wings between the rocks to the open sea, then no more do ye refrain from the path, but grip your oars well in your hands and cleave the sea's narrow strait, for the light of safety will be not so much in prayer as in strength of hands.'

So, following the king's suggestion, Jason set loose a dove, which flew between the rocks and made it through, losing only a few tail feathers. As soon as the rocks started to pull apart again, the Argonauts rowed 'with might and main' and succeeded in passing through the Straits into the Black Sea. By this action the spell was broken, and the islands never moved again.

Not all stories about doves talk of them in entirely peaceful terms. In Japan, for example, their supposed pugnacity has led them to be regarded as messengers of war rather than symbols of peace. One story tells how the mythical hero Yorimoto, hiding from his enemies in a hollow tree, was saved from discovery when two doves flew out of the tree, convincing his pursuers that no one else could possibly be inside. He later set up shrines to the gods of war, on which he depicted the birds that had saved him.

Nor are all stories equally complimentary. One less than flattering tale is told of two doves engraved on a stone slab in Jerusalem. It was believed that King Solomon (who could understand the language of the birds) one day overheard two doves talking to each other on the roof of the temple. One proclaimed that he was far more powerful than Solomon and could, with one blow of his foot, crush the temple. Solomon sent for the bird, and when it was brought before him he admonished it for being so conceited. The bird replied that he had been talking to his mate and that, as the king knew, it was necessary sometimes to boast before females in order to preserve one's self-respect. King Solomon, who had done his share of boasting to the Queen of Sheba, was highly amused. He ordered the bird to boast no more, then set him free. When the dove returned to its mate on the roof it told her that the king had been completely terrified and had begged him not to crush the temple. Solomon heard this lie and became so angry that he turned both doves into stone.

In several countries, such as Italy, Germany, Russia and Bohemia, the bird was highly esteemed and indeed revered, to the extent that to kill or eat a turtle dove was considered a sin. In parts of Wales, on the other hand, it was considered to be an unlucky bird until quite recently. It was especially ominous if one flew over a colliery, as this was believed to presage a disaster. Similarly, in the Channel Islands, keeping pet doves was thought unwise for people who had become betrothed, since the result would be a turbulent and difficult marriage.

This belief echoes the reality that doves are not monogamous birds. That said, there is also a conflicting strain of belief that holds that they are eternally faithful to their mates. One myth says that if a dove should lose its mate, it will only drink from a muddy puddle or after dark so that it does not have to see its dead partner in the reflection. This notion is referred to by Chaucer in his *Parlement of Fowles*, and by Elizabethan poet Sir Philip Sidney, who wrote:

> Time doth work what no man knoweth,
> Time doth us the subject prove,
> With time still affection groweth
> To the faithful turtledove.

Eagle
(Aquila chrysaetos)

Mainly sombre in colour, the eagle has a heavy bill and powerful claws. Its average wingspan is 150–210 cm. It inhabits mountainous regions and soars high on wind currents. This bird of prey feeds on mice, hares, foxes and fawns and can live for up to thirty years.

The eagle's place in folklore goes back thousands of years. Indeed, a number of early civilizations worshipped deities that took eagle form, and there is evidence from as early as 3000 BC that a Sumerian god of fertility, tempest and war known as Ningirsu was connected with the eagle.

Eagles crop up constantly in Greek mythology. One story concerns Periphas, a pious man, who was so devout that men built temples in his honour. This enraged Zeus, so he flung thunderbolts at the temples, reducing them to rubble, despite Apollo's appeals on Periphas' behalf. Later, Zeus surprised Periphas making love to his wife and turned him into an eagle. Periphas' wife was so distressed that she pleaded with Zeus to transform her into a bird as well so that she and her husband would not be separated. Touched by her pleas, Zeus turned her into a lammergeyer (a vulture) and, because Periphas had been such a pious man, decreed that the eagle should be king of the birds and permitted to approach his throne at any time. In time it became a symbol of Zeus.

A famous Greek myth tells how Zeus used an eagle as part of a particularly cruel punishment for the Titan Prometheus. Prometheus didn't have much respect for the gods, and in fact openly ridiculed Zeus, but it was for his indulgent treatment of mankind that he was punished so severely. Against the express wishes of Zeus, Prometheus stole fire from Mount Olympus and brought it to men in the hollow fennel wand he used as a staff. Enraged, Zeus had Prometheus carried off to Mount Caucasus, where he was chained to a rock so that Ethon the eagle could peck at his liver. As he was immortal, every day Prometheus' liver would grow back and every day the eagle would feast again. This punishment lasted for over twelve generations, until Heracles freed the Titan by shooting the eagle with an arrow.

In Roman mythology, which closely mirrored Greek mythology, the eagle similarly symbolized the chief of the gods, Jupiter. This fact probably helps to explain why, during the era of imperial Rome, live birds were used in the ceremony known as 'apotheosis', a ritual designed to symbolize the deification of a dead emperor. During the ceremony, a waxen image of the emperor would be burnt on a pyre, and a caged eagle would be hidden behind the blaze. At the climax, the bird would be released to carry the emperor's soul to the gods. The seventeenth-century poet John Dryden draws on this myth in the opening stanza of his poem on the death of Oliver Cromwell:

> Like eager Romans e'er all Rites were past,
> Did let too soon the sacred Eagle fly.

The eagle has strong associations with Christianity, and even today many lecterns in churches are in the shape of an eagle with outspread wings. The tradition behind this stems from the account of the divine throne given in Revelations (4: 6–7):

> And before the throne there was a sea of glass like unto crystal: and in the midst of the throne, and round about the throne, were four beasts full of eyes before and behind.
> And the first beast was like a lion, and the second beast like a calf, and the third beast had a face as a man, and the fourth beast was like a flying eagle.

The eagle is also used in Christian art to represent St John the Evangelist.

The power and fierceness of the eagle is echoed in its frequent folkloric associations with strength and valour. Over the centuries, the emblem of the eagle has been carried into battle on shields and banners in many countries: the most famous were probably the eagles surmounting the standards of Roman legions. Originally, the legions had four other emblems: the boar, the minotaur, the wolf and the horse, but in 104 BC the Roman general Gaius Marius abolished these so that the eagle could stand alone. It was said that if a pair of eagles appeared when a legion settled into its winter quarters, this was a particularly good omen.

Other cultures that have taken the eagle as their national

symbol include the Babylonians and the Persians. More recently, it was adopted by the French army during the first Napoleonic Empire. A heraldic eagle with two heads looking in opposite directions was the symbol in the nineteenth century of both the Austro-Hungarian Empire and imperial Russia.

Eagles have played a part in predicting the future, too. In the Snowdonian mountains of North Wales, in particular, eagles were observed with exceptional interest. If the birds soared and circled high in the air, this was said to portend victory, but if they flew low over the valleys uttering shrill cries, then death and disease were predicted. There is an old folk tale that tells of a great conference of eagles on Mount Snowdon, to which birds from as far afield as Cader Idris and Plynlimmon flocked. Once their deliberations were over, all the birds took off at the same time, causing a disastrous storm. Long after eagles had ceased to breed in Wales, local people could be heard to say, if the weather ever looked threatening, that the eagles were breeding storms on Mount Snowdon.

Seeing an eagle was invariably thought to be a favourable omen, but there was one rare event that was considered to foretell dire consequences: an eagle or other bird of prey being overcome by a lesser bird. This inversion of the natural order of things is referred to by Shakespeare in Act II of *Macbeth*, where, among other strange events observed after the murder of Duncan (including horses turning cannibal), it is observed how:

> On Tuesday last,
> A falcon, towering in her pride of place,
> Was by a mousing owl hawked at and killed.

While eagles are understandably considered to be strong and powerful birds, it is their vision that is often singled out for praise: 'eagle-eyed' is still a widely used phrase to describe someone who is incredibly meticulous and misses nothing. Interestingly, the expression arose from the myth that eagles could look directly at the sun without blinking. It was believed that females made their young look straight at the sun; if they were not able to do so, they were not considered to be true eagles and were thrown out of the nest. Shakespeare referred to this myth in *Henry VI, Part III* (Act II, Scene 1):

> Nay if thou be that princely eagle's bird
> Show thy descent by gazing 'gainst the sun.

Another myth claims that eagles never grow old because they are able to refresh their strength, hence the line in Psalm 103: 'thy youth is renewed like the eagle's.' The two ideas of renewal and the eagle's relationship with the sun come together in the belief that the eagle could place itself in the focus of the sun's rays, set its wings on fire and burn its old feathers away. The bird would then plunge into the sea or a pool of water from which it would arise, phoenix-like, with new feathers, new life and new strength. In his *Sefer ha-Qabbalah* (*Book of Tradition*), the twelfth-century Spanish historian and philosopher Rabbi Avraham ben David ha-Levi recorded this belief, adding that sometimes the eagle delayed its rejuvenation for too long and, not having the necessary strength to rise from the water, consequently drowned. Writing around the year 1250, Albertus Magnus, who was one of the Middle Ages' greatest advocates of the compatibility of religion and science and the first scholar to apply Aristotle's philosophy to Christian thought, described almost the same myth, but added his doubts as to its veracity:

> I can only consider this a miraculous occurrence, since in the two eagles which I kept I observed no changes of this sort; for they were tame and docile and moulted in the same manner as other birds of prey.

Another myth suggested that the eagle's power is very much linked to its beak, and that over time the upper half grows over the lower half, preventing the bird from eating. However, if the eagle pares the beak down by rubbing it against a rock, it can regain its health and strength.

Like the SWALLOW and the RAVEN, the eagle was believed to conceal a magic stone in its nest, the purpose of which was to alleviate the great difficulty the eagle was thought to experience when laying its eggs. The outer casing of the stone was supposed to be red or black and spotted with yellow, with a smaller stone inside the larger one. The stone's power to ease the bird's discomfort was thought to be transferable to women who experienced problems with childbirth, including those who had previously had miscarriages. If held against the woman's thigh during labour it was thought not only to make the delivery swift and easy but also to ensure that a strong, healthy baby would be born. So powerful was the stone's effect that it was essential not to keep it in contact with the woman for too long after the birth in case it caused a prolapse of the womb.

Naturally, anyone who was fortunate enough to possess an eagle stone found that it was much in demand, and in some instances a special box or bag was made to carry the stone from one household to another.

A strange myth about eagles comes from the Atlas mountains of North Africa, where it was believed that on occasion eagles would mate with foxes and produce monstrous offspring, known as *ṣṣāts* in the local Berber dialect, with the wings of a bird, the feet of a wolf and the tail of a serpent. There were some variations to this tale, the mother sometimes being a wolf or a hyena. A similar creature, the griffin, can be seen in many ancient Persian and Greek friezes; it had the body of a lion and the head and wings of an eagle. The combination perhaps came about because the lion was considered to be the king of the animals and the eagle the king of the birds. The griffin is a common charge (symbol) on heraldic coats of arms. Indeed, a number of heraldic creatures incorporate elements of an eagle: the calygreyhound resembles an antelope but has the forelegs and claws of an eagle and the rear legs and feet of an ox; the opinicus has the body and four legs of a lion, married with the neck and wings of an eagle and a short camel's tail; and the wyvern is a flying serpent, much like a dragon, but with two legs like an eagle's and a barbed tail.

One belief that has proved remarkably persistent is that eagles, particularly golden eagles, have in the past carried away human babies. Possibly the best-documented instance of this comes from Shetland and is described by Bobby Tulloch in *The Scots Magazine* (1978). His source was a fisherman who heard the details of the story from an old historian on Fetlar. In this case, the bird concerned was a white-tailed eagle which at the time (1790) bred on Shetland in some numbers. The tale goes as follows:

A crofter called William Anderson living on the north of the island of Unst was out cutting the hay with his wife. After a while she went into the croft to make a drink of tea leaving their baby, warmly wrapped in a thick shawl, lying in the field. The husband had moved further up the field when he looked round and saw a huge bird swoop down and with the baby clutched in its talons, fly away to the south. The parents and neighbours ran as far as they could but could only watch helplessly as the bird swept out over the sea towards the island of Fetlar. The pursuers then followed the eagle by fishing boat and landed on Fetlar where they quickly explained to the inhabitants the situation. The locals told them that there was a sea-eagle's eyrie on the high cliffs at Sail. Ropes were collected and an agile young boy called Robert Nicholson volunteered to be lowered down to the nest. When he reached it he found the baby, still wrapped in its shawl, lying between two eaglets. He was safely hauled up the cliff with the baby who was quite unhurt. Years later the rescuer Robert married the baby and by all accounts they lived very happily together with their descendants still living on Shetland today.

Given all the circumstantial detail, and the fact that the sea eagle is a particularly powerful bird, it is very tempting to believe that this account might have some basis in fact. Sadly, though, it is almost certainly pure fantasy.

Goose
(Anser anser)

Large waterbirds frequently found in flocks. Most legends probably refer to domesticated geese, which at one time were important food sources. The birds have high barking or honking calls and eat leaves, roots and seeds. Some breeds live up to twenty-three years.

The association between geese and humans stretches back thousands of years – there is evidence that they were being kept as domestic animals in Egypt by the time of the New Kingdom between 1530 and 1050 BC – so it is perhaps not surprising to find that they play a key role in the ritual and myth of many cultures. For the Romans, they were sacred to the goddess Juno, and enjoyed particularly high status because their warning cries were believed to have thwarted an attack on Rome by the Gauls in 390 BC. For the ancient Egyptians, they were associated with the earth god Seb. And in ancient China, a goose was considered to be a messenger between heaven and earth. In the thirteenth century, Pope Gregory IX inveighed against a group of Frisian peasants known as the Stedingers (meaning 'those living along a shore'), accusing them of devil worship. The object of their devotion was a god called Asmodi, who appeared to them in the form of a goose or duck. During these rites it was said that he enveloped them in darkness while they engaged in sexual orgies. The writer Edward A. Armstrong suggested that this was a fertility ceremony presided over by a pagan god, and it would seem to tie in with accounts of

'Berchta' or 'Bloody Bertha', an earth mother who was preceded by a flying goose.

Geese were widely sacrificed. Their bones have been found in pagan Swedish ship burials and as grave offerings. The ancient Koreans would drink a mixture of spirits and the blood of wild white geese, and the Chinese killed and ate geese at the summer solstice. The western tradition of eating roast goose at Michaelmas (29 September) may well have its origins in the sacrificial offerings of pagan times. It is certainly the case that the ancient Germans sacrificed geese to the chief of the gods, Odin, at the time of the autumn equinox – and Michaelmas and the autumn equinox fall very close to each other. In Britain, goose was eaten on special religious occasions, but there seems to have been a certain reluctance to eat it at other times. One suggestion is that, as with the avoidance of horse flesh, this reluctance dates back to a time when both geese and horses were regarded as objects of worship.

Geese were also eaten on St Martin's Night (11 November), an occasion on which the 'divination of the wishbone' or 'merry thought' took place: two people would pull the wishbone (in technical terms, the furcula) of the goose, and the person who broke off the larger piece could either make a wish or have the guarantee of good luck. A similar tradition grew up with chickens and turkeys, but since so many poultry are now served off the bone, this is a much rarer childhood ritual than it was even fifty years ago.

It was not just the wishbone that could be used for the purposes of divination. In fifteenth-century Bavaria, on the morning after St Martin's Day, when the goose had been eaten, the breastbone, which had been allowed to dry overnight, would be closely examined by the oldest and wisest peasant. He would try to foretell from the appearance of the bone whether the coming winter would be cold, wet or dry. The Teutonic Knights of Prussia even waged their wars according to the auguries divined from geese's breastbones.

In the Far East the goose was closely connected with marriage, and the practice of presenting a live wild goose as a nuptial gift is a very ancient one, it being the custom for the bridegroom's family to give the goose to the bride.

While these beliefs have been associated with many different species of goose, there is one persistent and rather bizarre belief that attached itself to one particular species: the barnacle goose.

Barnacle geese breed in the far north of the Arctic. They are winter visitors to Britain, where they tend to be largely concentrated in the Hebrides, the Solway Firth and the west coast of Ireland, although small numbers may be seen elsewhere around the coasts of England and Scotland. It is significant that the main centres of their winter sojourn lie precisely in those areas where traditions about them are particularly strong, namely the Western Isles and the west of Ireland.

The myth from which the bird derives its popular name is that the bird hatches from the barnacles that grow on rotting timber at the water's edge. The origin of the myth lies far back in time and persisted in some remote parts of Ireland until at least the beginning of the twentieth century. Writing in 1186 in his *Topographia Hiberniae* (*The Topography of Ireland*), Gerald de Barri, also known as Giraldus Cambrensis or Gerald of Wales, stated on his return from a tour in Ireland with Prince John that he had actually seen barnacle geese hatching from shells attached to waterlogged timbers:

They are produced from timber tossed along the sea and are at first like gum. Afterwards they hang down by their beaks as if they were seaweed attached to the timber and are surrounded by shells in order to grow more freely. Having thus in process of time been clothed with a strong coat of feathers, they either fall into the water or fly freely away into the air. They derive their food and growth from the sap of the wood or from the sea by a secret and most wonderful process of alimentation. I have frequently seen with my own eyes more than a thousand of these small birds hanging down by the seashore from one piece of timber, enclosed in their shells and already formed. They do not breed and lay eggs like other birds, nor do they ever hatch any eggs, nor do they seem to build nests in any corner of the earth. Hence bishops and religious men in some parts of Ireland do not scruple to dine off these birds at the time of fasting because they are not flesh or born of flesh.

Giraldus Cambrensis is notorious for being an unreliable recorder of events, but in this case his account accords well with the views of other contemporary naturalists, and indeed with that of the Catholic Church of the time. It was not until 1215 that Pope Innocent III issued an edict at the Fourth Lateran Council proclaiming that barnacle geese were not fish, and should not be eaten as such. That a papal edict was considered necessary shows how deeply rooted the conviction was that barnacle geese were not true birds.

Belief in the myth was revived in the sixteenth century when the otherwise reliable and competent naturalist Sir William Turner (c.1508–68) gave more or less the same account as Giraldus Cambrensis had given three hundred or so years earlier. He became convinced that it was true and wrote to the great Swiss naturalist Conrad Gesner (1516–65) with the following description:

There break out what seems like fungi; in these after a time the obvious shapes of birds become visible, then they are clad in feathers, then they come to live and fly.

Other naturalists of the period, such as Ulisse Aldrovandi (1522–1605), accepted the belief, and John Gerard in his *Herball* of 1597 gave an account of how he found some shells between Dover and Romney which contained 'Birds covered with soft downe and the shell open and the birds ready to fall out'. He also copied a picture from his contemporary Matthias de Lobel's *Plantarum Seu Stirpium Historia (History of Plants)*, modifying it to show the small birds more clearly.

So where does the myth originate? One recent commentator has traced it back to early Jewish writers, pointing out that there was widespread debate among Jewish scholars as to whether geese were fish or flesh, and even suggestions that there were actually birds that grew on trees. As a result there was considerable debate as to the ritual manner in which they should be slaughtered. One notable rabbi, Jacob Tam of Remeru, who died in 1171, decided that they should be killed as flesh.

But it was not only Jewish scholars who concerned themselves with the debate. In the tenth century AD, Ibrahim ibn Ahmed al-Turtushi, a diplomat from the Muslim part of Spain, made the following observations about a land that he called 'Shashin' (possibly Ireland):

There is something marvellous there such as is nowhere else in the world. On the seashore grow trees and from time to time the bank gives way and a tree falls into the sea. The waves toss it up and down so much that a white jelly is formed on it. This goes on until the jelly increases in size and assumes the shape of an egg. Then the egg is moulded in the form of a bird with nothing but both feet and bill from the wood. So it becomes a bird which scuttles in the sea about the surface of the water. It is never found alive but when the sea rises it is thrown back by the water on the shore where it is found dead. It is a black bird similar to the bird which is called the diver.

It is quite possible that Ibrahim ibn Ahmed was referring here to a species other than the barnacle goose, possibly the brent goose, which is a much more familiar sight on the south and east coasts of Britain, and was frequently mistaken for the barnacle goose. Another possibility, judging from the physical and behavioural attributes described by a number of writers in the Middle Ages, is that Ibrahim ibn Ahmed was describing the little auk. The little auk is largely black, it nests far to the north where it was almost certainly not seen by the naturalists of the day, and spends the non-breeding phase of its life cycle far out on the ocean. It only comes to shore during great gales, when many hundred, or even thousands, may be washed up on the land or on beaches. Being totally exhausted by the time that they reach the coast, almost all perish. The puffin, which was sometimes mistaken for the little auk, has also been referred to as 'half fish, half flesh'.

The myth that animals in various forms are born from trees was known in other parts of the world, such as India and the Middle East. Friar Odoric, who journeyed to India and China around the year 1318, wrote about a kind of tree which bore fruit similar to a melon, containing an animal like a young lamb. He also referred to trees found on the shores of the Irish Sea 'which at a certain time of the year do fall into the water and become birds'. The eleventh-century scholar al-Biruni described a tree, growing beside the Indian Ocean, with curled leaves that flew away as bees, while the twelfth-century Jewish writer Judah Hadasi wrote of trees on a mythical island in the Orient that produced maidens. There could possibly have been some connection here with the very suggestive-looking seeds of the coco de mer tree in the Seychelles, which sometimes drift far away on the ocean currents.

One goose-related expression that has entered the language is 'Don't kill the goose that lays the golden eggs'. Its origins are obscure, though it features in a fable by Aesop in which a man and his wife who are lucky enough to own a goose that lays golden eggs make the mistake of killing it because they greedily assume that the whole goose must be made of gold. However, Harold Bayley, in *The Lost Language of Symbolism* (1912), shows that the idea of a golden goose's egg is very ancient indeed:

The Hindus represent Brahma, the breath of life, as riding upon a goose and the Egyptians symbolised Seb, the father of Osiris, as a goose ... according to the Hindu theory of the creation the supreme spirit laid a golden egg resplendent as the sun and from the golden egg was born Brahma, the progenitor of the universe. The Egyptians had a similar story and described the sun as an egg laid by the primeval goose, in late times said to be a god. It is probably that our fairy tale of the goose that laid the golden egg is a relic of this very ancient mythology.

Hoopoe
(Upupa epops)

Medium-sized, mainly fawn-coloured bird with a very large crest that is sometimes raised like a fan, particularly when the bird is excited. It has a very distinctive flapping flight and a soft cooing call. Very rare in Britain, though the birds can sometimes be sighted there if they overshoot on their route from Africa to Europe.

With its striking plumage, long curved bill and crest, the hoopoe is hard to miss, and, like many other birds of conspicuous appearance, it has gathered around itself fables both complimentary and critical, particularly from its native haunts in Africa, southern Europe and the Middle East.

Many of the myths concern the distinctive call of the hoopoe (from which the bird gets its name). There was, for example, a legend in southern Germany that the hoopoe and the bittern used to keep cattle. The bittern pastured his animals in rich, lush fields near the marsh where he lived; the hoopoe, by contrast, kept his on high barren hills. The bittern's cows grew fat and lazy, while the hoopoe's became thin and weak. When the time came to gather the animals in, those belonging to the bittern were so well fed and frisky they refused to come, however often the bittern called, 'Herum, herum' ('Here, here'). The hoopoe's cattle, by contrast, were so emaciated that despite its continual call of 'Up, up, up' they were unable to move. Having failed miserably as farmers, the birds never kept cattle again, but they did retain the same calls.

In Brittany, it was held that the hoopoe and the WOODPECKER were close friends and companions. The story goes that they decided to leave their native country and fly to new lands across the sea. On the journey, the woodpecker became very tired and kept dozing off. In order to keep his friend awake, the hoopoe continuously called, 'Hoop-hoop-hoop,' and thus prevented him from falling into the sea. When they arrived safely, the woodpecker was so grateful to his friend for his help that he excavated a fine big hole in a tree for the hoopoe to make his nest in. To this day, many hoopoes use old woodpecker's holes for their nesting sites.

In some parts of Germany it was believed that the CUCKOO once had a crest like the hoopoe has now, until the time both birds were invited to a wedding at which the hoopoe was asked to give the bride away. Wishing to look more imposing, it begged the cuckoo to be allowed to borrow its crest. The cuckoo agreed, and the hoopoe, impressed by how handsome it then looked, refused to give it back. Thoroughly enraged, the cuckoo called repeatedly, 'Kluku, kluku' ('You knave, you knave'), to which the hoopoe replied, 'Jdu, jdu, jdu' ('I'm coming, I'm coming'). In Bavaria, the hoopoe is believed to be the cuckoo's servant in much the same way that in parts of Britain the WRYNECK is said to be the cuckoo's mate.

Like so many other birds which migrate to Europe in the spring, the hoopoe's time of arrival was believed to foretell the quality of the harvest for that year. If it was heard calling before the vines begin to ripen then it was assumed that the grape harvest would be plentiful and the wine of good quality. In Chinese mythology, the hoopoe was similarly seen as the harbinger of spring and was considered a particularly auspicious bird because of its beautiful appearance. By contrast, in Sweden it was known as the army bird, its cries being thought to portend the coming of war or famine.

At one time, many people in southern Germany held that, like the woodpecker, the hoopoe knew the secret of the spring-wort (a magical plant that could open locks and remove barriers). In the Tyrol, the bird was credited with special magical properties, and it was believed that people who carried the bird's eyes with them would be loved and admired by everyone they encountered. It was long thought that carrying the bird's head around guarded against evil spells and also ensured success in the law courts (though this latter attribute sounds to be more an urban than a rural tradition).

There is a great body of lore regarding the medicinal properties of the hoopoe, practically all of which seems to have served some function or other. A fairly typical account is given in *Syrian Anatomy, Surgery and Therapeutics* by E. A. W. Budge, published in 1913:

Kill it with a piece of money on which is [written] the name of God. Take a new vessal, and throw the bird into it, and with it put two drachms of red lime and one drachm of wood ashes, and boil it in water until it is parboiled. Then take out the bird. Put the head on one side, and the right pinion on one side. Remove one section of it, and place it in a vessel of wine, and whosoever drinketh thereof will become drunk. The left pinion is good for the man who is in thrall to his wife; remove one section of the bird and set it in oil and let the man drink, and he shall be free.

Tie up the right shoulder in a piece of new rag and hang it over a woman who is ill in her body and she shall have relief. Steep its tongue in rose water for five days and tie it up in a buffalo skin and hold it in thy hand and the dogs will not bark at thee. Dry its skull and macerate it in oil and rub it on any part of the body thou wisheth and it will destroy the hair. Dry a bone of the back in the shade and pound it and pour oil of violets over it and if thee rubbest it on any part of the body the hair will grow. Having salted the heart of this bird with Indian salt tie it in a lion's skin and give it to a woman whose child will not come forth from her.

Let her grasp it in her left hand and the child will descend from her womb straightaway. If a man drink the lungs of the bird in a very bitter water, he will not be able to attempt to copulate all the days of his life. If its liver be pounded and mixed with crocus, it is good for the lungs and the heart and the spleen. If a man hangeth up the left wing over himself on the night of his wedding nothing will be done. Mix its right side with Spahul eye paint and smear thine eyes therewith and everyone who seeth thee will receive thee gladly.

The hoopoe is still highly regarded in the Arab world, where, because of its supposed medicinal powers, it is often referred to as 'the doctor', besides being credited with the gift of water divination. It was also believed by the ancient Egyptians that in gratitude for their upbringing, young hoopoes made a nest for and looked after parent birds when they grew old and infirm.

The Persians had a particular regard for the hoopoe. One of the most famous mystic poets of Iran, Farid ud-Din Attar (*c.*1142–*c.*1220), wrote in his masterpiece *Mantiq at-Tayr* (*The Conference of Birds*) about a hoopoe who is the leader of a group of birds undertaking a journey to enlightenment. Each bird has a special significance in Islamic culture: the NIGHTIN-GALE, for example, symbolizes love; the parrot is a seeker after the fountain of immortality; and the PEACOCK is the embodiment of the fallen soul, in alliance with Satan. The hoopoe leads these birds on their long and arduous journey, and along the way many fall by the wayside. Eventually, only thirty birds arrive at their destination, the land of the *Simorgh*, which means both a mysterious phoenix-like bird in Iranian mythology and 'thirty birds' (*si morgh*). What they discover in this land is nothing more than their own reflections in the lake – a powerful illustration of the poet's view that the true nature of God is within us.

There are also a number of legends that connect hoopoes with King Solomon. One such tale begins with Solomon travelling in the desert and finding himself overwhelmed by the great heat – so much so that he is forced to lie down. A flock of hoopoes come and shade him from the sun, and as a reward he bestows their fine crests upon them. Another version of this story tells how Solomon at first grants the hoopoes crowns of gold, but because men then begin to hunt and kill them for their riches, the hoopoes plead with Solomon that they might have a beautiful crest instead.

Much opprobrium has been heaped upon the hoopoe on account of its extremely dirty and smelly nesting holes. One story that seeks to explain this comes from Eastern Europe and tells how, in the beginning, when God gave all the birds different foods, millet, barley and wheat were all offered in turn to the hoopoe – who refused all three. At this point the Almighty became exasperated and said that as the hoopoe would not eat good food, it would have to take the worst and eat only excrement. In fact, the hoopoe's diet consists almost entirely of insects and small lizards but because carrion and manure contain large numbers of grubs and flies, it spends much of its time probing and searching through the filth, even though it doesn't eat it. These peculiar feeding habits probably explain why in the Old Testament (Leviticus 11: 9) the bird was included in a list of unclean birds.

House Sparrow
(Passer domesticus)

Universally recognized bird that has spread throughout the world. Numbers have declined rapidly in Western Europe in the last decade or so – in many places by as much as 50 per cent. Adaptable little birds, living in both cities and the countryside, they can have up to three broods each year. Being highly sociable, they roost in groups in shrubs and hedgerows and their combined chirping is a familiar sound at dusk.

All over the world, sparrows are considered to be pests: they are notorious for stealing spilt corn, especially when the seed has just been sown. Chairman Mao famously used people power in 1958 to destroy the sparrow population of China, every peasant being ordered to keep banging and shouting to prevent the sparrows from landing, until they fell from the sky, dead from exhaustion. Myth and legend, sadly, take a similarly dim view of them.

In Bohemia, there were supposed to be three magical ways to thwart sparrows' thievery. The first was to place a splinter of wood taken from a coffin in the field containing the freshly sown corn; this was thought to keep the birds at bay. The second was designed to prevent sparrows from eating corn stored in a barn; all it required was for the farmer to place a bone from a grave at the entrance of the building. Finally, there was a special method of sowing the corn that was thought to protect the seed from the birds. All sowers had to do was keep three

seeds of corn beneath their tongue as they walked up and down the field scattering the seed, and then, when they reached the end of each furrow, they had to spit out the seeds, saying, 'In the name of the Father and the Son and of the Holy Ghost.' This last spell was thought to be so powerful that no sparrow would dare to come into the field once it was cast.

The bird was associated closely with Christianity, but in an entirely negative way. There is an ancient story that tells how all the birds in the Garden of Gethsemane tried to divert the mob from the place where Jesus knelt in prayer. All, that is, except for the sparrows, whose constant chirpings drew attention to his whereabouts. As a result of this betrayal, Jesus cursed the sparrows and decreed that henceforth their flesh would be unclean. It could be argued that this edict worked to the sparrow's advantage as it meant that Christians would neither touch nor eat the bird.

There is a further explanation of the ignominy suffered by

sparrows that relates to their behaviour during the Crucifixion
It was believed that SWALLOWS sought to save Jesus from
suffering, first by stealing the nails he was to be crucified with
and hiding them from his executioners, then by calling out
prematurely that he was dead. But sparrows were thought to
have put paid to both these ruses, first by finding the nails and
bringing them back, and second by repeatedly calling out that
he still lived. As a punishment for their spite, Jesus decreed
that sparrows should for ever be unwelcome guests in any
home and that should one enter a house this would be an ill
omen.

Harbingers of death

For thousands of years people have believed that it is
possible to predict the future by observing the way in
which particular birds behave. All the following were
believed to be sure indications of an imminent death:

- Hearing a curlew's call at night, or a plover's call in
  the morning
- Hearing an owl's screech or a raven's croak
- A pigeon settling on a house
- A wild bird – particularly a robin – being seen in the
  house or tapping at a window
- Rooks deserting a rookery
- Seeing three swans flying together

The view that sparrows are unlucky has been recorded in many parts of Britain, particularly in Kent. Here it was believed that if a sparrow was captured, it had to be killed immediately, or the catcher would very soon die. It was also thought to be a particularly bad omen if a sparrow flew at a window, as this was believed to portend the imminent death of someone within the house.

Like many other species of birds, the sparrow provided useful material for the augurs of ancient Greece. It was recorded that when on their way to attack Troy at the start of the Trojan War, the Achaean fleet put into the port of Aulis in Greece. There a serpent was seen to catch and eat eight young sparrows and an adult bird. From these auguries, Calchas, the principal soothsayer, correctly divined that the war with Troy would last for over nine years.

Kingfisher
(Alcedo atthis)

A bright jewel of a bird, which skims over the water in a flash of blue and orange. It is able to see well in the air and underwater because its eyes have oval lenses. It dives for small fish, but will also eat crayfish, frogs and insects.

The kingfisher's spectacular colouring is the subject of many myths and legends, not least of which is the conviction held in Brittany that the bird could glow in the dark. One story, set in

the time of Noah's Flood, tells how the bird's plumage was originally dull and grey. After several weeks of drifting, Noah released the dull-coloured kingfisher from the ark and allowed it to fly free and find land. The bird was so relieved to be released after having been confined for so long, it climbed up and up into the sky until, finally, it went so high it took on the blue of the heavens. It then flew so near to the sun that the heat scorched its breast and it was forced to douse its smouldering feathers by diving into the water beneath.

It was at this point that the bird remembered it had been let out by Noah to search for dry land, but when it tried to catch up with the ark it could no longer find it. (This was because once the ark had landed on Mount Ararat, Noah had dismantled it in order to build a house from the wood.) The kingfisher grew more and more agitated and flew hither and thither over the water calling for its master – which is why the bird still flies low along rivers.

Because the kingfisher's nest is so well hidden in tunnels by river banks, there was considerable speculation as to its nesting habits; hence the following rather peculiar description by the usually more rational philosopher Aristotle in *The History of Animals*:

Its nest is like sea balls, the things that go by the name of sea foam; only the colour is not the same. The colour of the nest is light red and the shape is that of the long necked gourd. The nests are longer than the largest sponge, though they vary in size, they are roofed over and a great part of them is solid and a great part hollow. If you use a sharp knife it is not easy to cut the nest through; but if you cut it and at the same time bruise it with your hand it will soon crumble to pieces. The opening is small, just enough for a tiny entrance, so that even if the nest is upset the sea does not enter in; the hollow channels are like those in sponges. It is not known for certain of what material the nest is constructed; it is possibly made of the backbones of the gar-fish; for, by the way, the bird lives on fish.

Like so many birds, kingfishers have played an important role in folk medicine. Supposedly, their particular attribute was that not only did their bodies not decompose, but they also possessed the power to prevent other materials decaying. The twelfth-century chronicler Giraldus Cambrensis, who tended towards the fantastical, wrote:

> It is remarkable in these little birds that if they are preserved in a dry place when dead, they never decay and if they are put among clothes or other articles they preserve them from the moth and give them a pleasant odour. What is still more wonderful – if when dead they are hung up by their beaks in a dry situation, they change their plumage every year as if they were restored to life, as though the vital spark still survived and vegetated through some mysterious remains of its energy.

The kingfisher was also credited with possessing the power to enrich whoever owned the dead bird and to grant grace and loveliness to any woman who wore its feathers. For their part, the Tartars of Eastern Europe and central Asia believed kingfisher feathers could be turned into powerful love talismans. The method was to throw plucked kingfisher feathers into water, collect all those that floated, and then stroke the hapless object of affection with one of them. Such superstitions must have made life dangerous for the bird – many must have been killed for the supposedly magical effects of their feathers.

During the Middle Ages, a strange belief arose that if a dead kingfisher was hung up in a house by its bill and suspended from a length of thread, then its breast would be sure to turn in the direction from which the wind was about to blow. Sir Thomas Browne, the English Renaissance philosopher whose writings display a deep curiosity about the natural world, decided to test the truth of this by suspending two birds together. Perhaps not surprisingly, he found that they generally ended up facing in opposite directions. Even so, the practice of using dead kingfishers as weather forecasters continued into the early twentieth century, and it is referred to both by Christopher Marlowe in his play *The Jew of Malta* and by Shakespeare in *King Lear*, where in Act II, Scene 2 Kent speaks of those who:

> Renege, affirm, and turn their halcyon beaks
> With every gale and vary of their masters ...

Halcyon was the Greek word for kingfisher and is connected with the mythological story of Halcyone, the wife of Ceyx, King of Trachis. Ceyx was about to make a long sea voyage, and when he came to take his leave of Halcyone, they both had a presentiment that they would never meet again. Despite this, every day they were apart, Halcyone laid out clothes for her husband, believing that these would act as a talisman to bring her loved one home safely. As time went by, she became increasingly distressed, not least because in those days death by drowning was particularly feared: it was thought that the soul was composed of fire and air and so would be out of its element in water, and without a proper grave it would not be able to pass into its resting place in Hades.

Ceyx's ship had indeed been wrecked, but Halcyone had no way of knowing what had happened to her husband until Hera, the queen of immortals, took pity on her and sent Morpheus, the god of dreams, to tell her what had happened. He appeared to her in the guise of her husband, and when she awoke she rushed down to the shore to find the body of Ceyx washed up on the water's edge. The gods were so moved by her grief that they changed Ceyx and Halcyone into kingfishers to live for ever by the waterside, eternally faithful, destined never to take another mate should one of the pair die.

It was also believed that the gods granted the pair a fortnight of calm seas during the winter. In Western Europe this period, which took place around the time of St Martin's Day (11 November), became known as the 'halcyon days' – an expression that still survives in English to describe a period of calm, beautiful weather at any time of the year. And while the link between St Martin's Day and halcyon weather has generally been forgotten, one local name for the kingfisher, St Martin's bird (in France, *martin-pêcheur*), preserves the connection.

Lapwing
(Vanellus vanellus)

A mainly black-and-white wader, also known as the peewit (lapwing refers to the sound its wings make in flight and peewit to its call). The birds are migratory and like to eat worms and insects; they feed nocturnally on moonlit nights. A group of lapwings is called a 'deceit'.

Lapwings are rather beautiful and harmless birds, and yet in legend they have developed an unaccountably bad reputation.

A typical tale, which originated in Sweden, relates how the lapwing was once a handmaid to the Virgin Mary. One day the maid was discovered stealing a pair of scissors; her punishment was to be turned into a bird with a forked tail that looked like it had been snipped by scissors, and compelled to cry, 'Tyvit, tyvit' ('I stole, I stole').

A more familiar myth, this time originating in Denmark, tells of a time when Jesus as a child went for a walk and met an old woman who was baking bread in a large oven. She asked him to chop some wood for her and in return she would give him a piece of cake. He did as he was asked and the old lady broke off a minute piece of dough and put it in the oven. Immediately it grew into a full-sized cake. The greedy woman,

surprised by the size of the cake, refused to give it all to Jesus. Angered by such thriftiness, Jesus turned her into a lapwing, doomed to weep between heaven and earth for the rest of time. This tale is very similar to stories told about the black WOOD-PECKER and the eagle OWL, and it is probable that they share a common ancestry.

Like several other birds, the lapwing was supposed to have been present at the Crucifixion. One story tells of how three birds appeared to Jesus as he hung from the Cross. First came the STORK, who cried, 'Strengthen him! Strengthen him!'; then came the SWALLOW, who tried to remove the thorns from his crown; and last came the lapwing who flew around the Cross shrieking, 'Let him suffer! Let him suffer!' The stork and the swallow were blessed by Jesus and became beloved of mankind, while the lapwing was condemned for all eternity.

A myth originating from Russia also condemns the lapwing, but in the context of the Creation rather than the Crucifixion. It relates that when God created the world, he wished to fill with water all the places that would become seas, rivers and lakes. Accordingly, he ordered all the birds to carry water to these places, and all duly obeyed with the sole exception of the lapwing. As a punishment for its defiance, God decreed it would never be allowed to drink from a river or a lake but only from puddles and cavities under stones.

The lapwing was also thought to have displeased King Solomon, having not appeared at an assembly of the birds ordered by the great king. In this instance, however, the lapwing was able to exonerate itself, its excuse being that it had been far away at the time, visiting the Queen of Sheba. Rather than condemn it, Solomon decided instead to employ the lapwing as a messenger between himself and the queen's court.

One myth from the Middle East shows the bird in a more favourable light. It tells how the lapwing was once a beautiful princess who loved her only brother deeply. One day, after he had been absent for a long time on a journey, she was informed quite wrongly that he had returned. She was so anxious to bring him some refreshment that she snatched up a pot of hot milk from the fire and placed it on her head, rushing out to meet him and disregarding the burn she received from the scalding vessel. For years she searched in vain for her brother until finally Allah took pity on her and turned her into a lapwing in order to make her quest easier. To this day, some Middle Eastern women run out of their houses when they hear the lapwing calling and hurl a bowlful of water into the air to help the bird ease the pain of its scalded head.

From Denmark comes a story that links the lapwing with the green sandpiper. It recounts how the souls of old maids are changed into lapwings while those of bachelors enter into green sandpipers. As the birds fly over the moors the lapwings call, 'Hvi vi doit, hvi vi doit' ('Why wouldn't you?'), to which the green sandpipers reply, 'Fo we turr, fo we turr' ('Because we dare not'). The belief that the birds represent human souls has also been recorded in Britain. In rural areas, it was formerly believed that lapwings were the souls of the dead who remained on earth because something troubled them.

Shakespeare makes reference to two strange beliefs concerning the lapwing. The first, in *The Comedy of Errors* (Act V, Scene 2) – 'Far from her nest the lapwing cries away'

– refers to the view that the lapwing drew predators from its nest by flying away and calling loudly at some distance from the nest. Somewhat unfairly, this led the bird to be associated with insincerity. The second reference, in *Hamlet* (Act V, Scene 2) – 'This lapwing runs away with the shell on his head' – reflects the belief that newly hatched lapwings flew away from the nest with shell still stuck to their heads. By analogy this image came to describe a person who rushed ahead with something when they had very little experience.

Magpie
(Pica pica)

A striking member of the crow family, the magpie is metallic green and black with brilliant white underparts. Its long tail, which is very prominent in flight, is flaunted when on the ground – it has a very strutting walk. Magpies are often viewed as predators, eating other birds' eggs and fledglings, but they also play their part in pest control, eating insects and small rodents.

Magpies may be handsome, swashbuckling birds, but over the centuries they have developed a reputation both for being thieves and for being rather sinister – certainly in Britain. Even today, many people believe in the significance of seeing one or more magpies; hence the following traditional rhyme:

One for sorrow
Two for joy
Three for a girl
Four for a boy
Five for silver
Six for gold
Seven for a secret never to
be told.

An older version of the rhyme, but one which is still remembered, is:

One for sorrow
Two for mirth
Three for a wedding
Four for a birth
Five for heaven
Six for hell
Seven you'll see the de'il
himsel'.

Many variations of this rhyme have been recorded over the years; indeed, almost every region of Britain has its own version, particularly of the last two lines.

To counter the potential ill

luck occasioned by the sight of a single magpie, various rituals and counter-spells developed. In parts of the north of England, it was thought prudent either to make the sign of the cross or to raise one's hat or bow to the bird (this belief is still widely held in the West Riding of Yorkshire). It was also believed that reciting a rhyme, while making the sign of the cross, would ward off bad luck:

> I cross the magpie
> The magpie crosses me,
> Bad luck to the magpie
> And good luck to me.

Bad luck

Although bad luck is usually associated with particular species of birds, it can apply to birds in general in particular circumstances. Finding a dead bird on the path leading to your house, for example, was once, perhaps not surprisingly, counted an ill omen. Bringing birds' eggs into the house was also considered to be bad luck, although this presumably cannot have applied to chickens' eggs. And one rather obscure belief suggests that if birds settle on a property whose owner has the same name, then only bad luck will follow – particularly unfortunate if your name happens to be Robin Rook.

In other places it was the custom to cross one's feet or to spit in the direction of the bird, saying, 'Devil, devil, I defy thee.' In Suffolk, the advice was to face the bird and say, 'I spit on thee, brother.' Spotting a magpie flying in the opposite direction to the sun was regarded as a particularly bad omen, but it could be countered by calling out to the bird, 'Bad luck to the bird that goes widdershins [anticlockwise].' A less alarming superstition, and also the oldest one recorded, dating back to the twelfth century, is the belief that the sound of a chattering magpie foretells the coming of a stranger.

In contrast to the dislike and mistrust of the magpie felt in many parts of Britain, in Sussex it was considered a good omen if a magpie perched on the roof of a house. This belief was based on the premise that a wise magpie would never fall into the trap of resting on a building which was structurally unsafe. It was similarly held that a tree with a magpie's nest would never fall.

This idea that the magpie could be a force for evil but might also be a force for good was linked in Central Europe to its black and white plumage. Here it was believed that the bird was induced to do good by a kindly white fairy, or evil by a malignant black being. It was also believed in some parts that the magpie was the offspring of the DOVE and the RAVEN, the dove representing the positive aspects of the magpies's personality and significance, and the raven the negative.

The magpie also had an important role to play in Christian myth, not least in the well-known legend that it did not enter the ark with the other birds but instead sat on the roof, cackling as the world drowned. Such callous behaviour did not win it many friends. To make matters worse, it was also said that the magpie refused to go into full mourning after the Crucifixion and so was cursed by being unable to lay an egg unless she had suspended herself from a branch nine times in succession.

In Sweden, if the bird's neck feathers were seen to be moulting, the country folk would say that the magpie had gone to hell to help the devil carry his hay and that the yoke had caused the damage. There is a similar story in the South of France. In Scotland they went one further, the magpie becoming known as 'the devil's bird'. Here it was believed that the bird possessed a drop of human blood on its tongue that gave it the gift of human speech. The satanic connection continued in the belief that should a cross be cut into the bark of a tree in which a magpie built its nest, the bird would have no choice but to desert it.

The magpie is one of the few birds that builds more than a cup-shaped nest – it is, in fact, the largest bird in Britain to have a completely domed nest. An explanation for this is given in the story that the magpie alone knew the secret of building the perfect nest and, as a result, many other birds came to it for guidance. The magpie obliged and began its demonstration by laying two sticks across each other, then covering them with moss and feathers. At each stage of the construction, however, it was interrupted by the other birds saying they knew how to do that particular task already. Eventually the magpie flew off in frustration, leaving the other birds to their own devices.

A further belief about the magpie's nest was that it was always built near the source of a magic plant that had the power to sever iron or stone. In parts of France, it was thought that the magpie left its nest secured by sealing the entrance with sharp thorns. When it returned, it was thought to bring with it a few leaves of the magic plant, as, on contact with the plant, the thorns would melt away and allow the bird to enter with ease.

Magpies generally don't feature much in fok medicine, but around Dresden in Germany it was believed that a broth made of boiled magpie would cure epilepsy. However, a few dozen miles away in the Austrian Tyrol, that same broth was thought to turn the drinker mad.

Nightingale
(Luscinia luscinia)

A small member of the warbler family, which has russet upper parts, a broad tail, and is grey-brown below. Its preferred habitat is deciduous woods with dense undergrowth. It is notable for its beautiful song whose notes rise and fall in succession. Contrary to popular belief, nightingales don't just sing at night, but their song is more difficult to distinguish in daylight hours owing to competition from other birds and everyday ambient noise.

The nightingale may be a somewhat furtive and skulking bird with drab plumage, but what it lacks in physical beauty it makes up for with its recognizable and evocative song. Italian legend seeks to explain both attributes by suggesting that when God created the birds, the nightingale, being a very shy bird, came forward last, by

which time God had, unfortunately, run out of bright colours for its plumage. Not wishing to let the bird go away unrewarded he gave the nightingale the loveliest voice of all.

The sound of a nightingale singing in the quiet of the night is unforgettable, and perhaps as a result is the subject of a great body of folklore. St Francis of Assisi, the founder of the Franciscan Order, who had a great reputation for his affinity with animals and birds, was said to have sung duets with the nightingale. In France, there is a myth that originally the blindworm and the nightingale had one eye each. When the nightingale was invited to a wedding, it asked to borrow the blindworm's eye for the day so that it might look its best. After the wedding, the nightingale refused to return the eye and was thereafter compelled to remain awake all night in case the worm should try to get it back again. A further story which attempted to explain the nightingale's wakefulness was that the bird once overslept while roosting on a vine, and its feet became entangled in the growing tendrils. To prevent such a thing happening again, it sings all night to keep awake.

In Westphalia, the peasants believed that the nightingale was once a shepherdess who tantalized her lover by constantly postponing their wedding day. Eventually, he became so infuriated that he cursed her, changing her into a nightingale and condemning her to remain awake until the Day of Judgement. It was held that the bird's cries at night are the shepherdess calling to the dog that helps her guard her sheep.

Because the song of the nightingale is both pure and mournful, it's perhaps not surprising that various stories about it involve a forlorn hero or heroine being turned into a nightingale so that they can for ever express their grief in song. Greek mythology, for example, tells of the wicked Aedon, Queen of Thebes. She had only one child, a son called Itylus, but her sister-in-law Niobe had six sons and six daughters and she was insanely jealous of her – so jealous, in fact, that she resolved to kill some of Niobe's children. Because Itylus generally slept on the same couch as the other children, on the night Aedon planned to carry out her evil deed she told her son to sleep somewhere else. Tragically, he forgot, and so his mother killed him by mistake. She was so distraught with grief that Zeus took pity on her and turned her into a nightingale so that her remorse could be expressed in song for ever.

Perhaps the most famous Greek myth concerning nightingales is that of Philomela. Shakespeare referred to it in his poem *The Rape of Lucrece*, with the lines:

> Come, Philomel, that sing'st of ravishment,
> Make thy sad grave in my dishevell'd hair.

These imply that the bird's song is desolate because it is bewailing its lost virginity. However, this is only one part of the Greek story, which is a classic tale of betrayal and woe.

Procne and Philomela were the daughters of Pandion, King of Athens, and Procne was married off to her father's ally Tereus, King of Thrace. The couple moved away, had a son called Itys and were for the most part happy. Procne, however, longed for her sister, and so her husband offered to sail to Athens and escort Philomela back to Thrace to visit her sister and nephew. The journey was long, and during the return leg Tereus fell in love with his sister-in-law and raped her. Immediately regretting his actions and terrified that Philomela would betray him to his wife, Tereus cut out her tongue and hid her away in his dungeon. When he returned to his wife he simply told her that her sister had died. Although unable to speak, Philomela was able to weave a message into a cloak which was smuggled to Procne. Appalled at her sister's fate, Procne freed Philomela, and together they plotted a terrible revenge. First, Procne killed her son, then she disguised his flesh as food and gave it to Tereus to eat. As he swallowed the last mouthful, she revealed to him what she had done before fleeing with Philomela. Outraged and distraught, Tereus set off to pursue and kill the sisters, but at this point Zeus intervened and turned them all into birds. Tereus became a HOOPOE, Philomela became a SWALLOW and Procne a nightingale. When the Roman poet Ovid later retold the story, he amended the original, making Procne the swallow and Philomela the nightingale. It is Ovid's version that has persisted, and poets ever since have referred to Philomela as the beautiful singer and to the nightingale as 'philomel'.

As well as myths seeking to explain the origin of the nightingale's song, there are also stories that speculate about where the bird makes its nest. In Britain, it was at one time held that the nightingale was frightened of water; it would cross the sea at the narrowest possible point and not settle in areas too far away from its point of entry. Another belief claimed that the nightingale bred only where cowslips grew, and yet another that hops were essential for the birds to breed. This latter idea may have arisen because hops were at one time widely grown in Kent, and, as it happens, Kent has always tended to have quite a large population of nightingales.

The nightingale's song has not proved universally popular, particularly among the more saintly members of society. No nightingales are supposed to sing in Havering-atte-Bower in Essex, for example, because they were specifically asked not to do so by Edward the Confessor, who didn't want them to interrupt his meditations. Similarly, the sixteenth-century writer Andrew Boorde describes in his *Book of Knowledge* how a hermit living in a forest in Sussex took steps to ensure that his prayers should not be interrupted by cursing the nightingales:

> In the forest of Saint Leonards in Southsex there doth never singe nightingale althoughe the foreste rounde about in tyme of the years is replenished with nightingales; they wyl syng round aboute the foreste and never within the precincte of the forests as divers keepers of the foreste and other credible persons dwellying there dyd shew me.

That favourite figure of folklore, King Solomon, has also been connected with the nightingale. The story goes that the other birds complained to the king, saying that the nightingale kept them all awake by insisting on singing through the night. Solomon asked the nightingale to explain itself, and the bird responded by saying that it only sang to win the heart of its lover. This impressed the king, who had himself written some beautiful love songs, so he ruled in favour of the nightingale, who was allowed to continue singing sweetly through the night.

In the Middle Ages, it was widely believed that nightingales had a great fear of snakes, and would roost with their breasts against a thorn to try and keep themselves awake. Writing in *Enquiries into Vulgar and Common Errors* (Part III), in around 1650, Sir Thomas Browne, with his usual common sense, questioned this particular myth, suggesting that it might have come about because nightingales often nest in dense and thorny thickets, possibly to defend their nests from being raided by snakes and vermin. This nesting habit could also well have led to the widely known legend of the nightingale and the rose. In the Middle East it was believed that the nightingale was the rose's lover, and that it was the song of the nightingale, perched upon the branches of the rose bush, that caused the buds to open. Eventually, in an ecstasy of passion aroused by the perfume of the rose, the nightingale would fall unconscious to the ground. This story was taken up by Oscar Wilde in his story 'The Nightingale and the Rose' (1888).

There is a great deal of folklore in Britain and continental Europe that connects the nightingale with the CUCKOO, in part because both birds tend to arrive at a similar time each spring. If the nightingale was heard before the cuckoo it was thought to be a particularly good omen, because the nightingale's call represented success in love, whereas the cuckoo's call represented mocked love. John Milton (1608–74) had this in mind when he wrote 'To the Nightingale':

> Thy liquid notes that close the eye of day,
> First heard before the shallow cuckoo's bill,
> Portend success in love.

One folk tale tells of a dispute between the nightingale and the cuckoo over whose song was better. Because of its large ears, a donkey was chosen to be the judge of the contest. The donkey chose the cuckoo as the winner, and the nightingale was so incensed that it now sings day and night to convince mankind that its song is better.

At one time it was thought that the heart and eyes of a nightingale placed in a bed kept the occupant awake, and that if these parts were dissolved and given to someone to drink they would never again sleep properly. In Brittany, they believed that if a person ate a nightingale's heart they would only sleep for two hours a night, which was the length of time the bird itself slept, but that if the wind changed within twenty-four hours of the medicine's ingestion, then they would run the risk of madness.

Nightjar
(Caprimulgus europaeus)

A small bird with huge eyes, a wide, flat beak and grey/brown mottled and barred plumage, the nightjar is mostly nocturnal and so is rarely seen, though it is often heard. Its silent flight is light and buoyant with many twists and turns. Its song is long and churring, and rises and falls in pitch.

Given its nocturnal activities and its silent, ghostlike, twisting flight, it is perhaps not surprising that the nightjar has attracted a considerable body of adverse folklore. Man, being primarily a creature adapted to a daylight existence, has always had an instinctive and deep-rooted fear of night creatures, and it is no doubt this fear that ultimately lies behind the stories equating the nightjar and its call with witchcraft and death.

As the bird is so well camouflaged, it often reveals itself only by its strange, almost disembodied song. This low churring rising and falling sometimes ceases suddenly, while at other times it appears to run down like a clockwork toy. Early observers likened the song to the sound of a whirring spinning wheel; hence such popular names for the bird as 'spinner' or 'wheelbird'.

One of the commonest myths about the nightjar was that it sucked the milk from cows and goats. First reported by Aristotle, this belief subsequently spread right across Europe, resulting in such names for the bird as the German *Ziegenmelker*, the

Spanish *chotacabras gris* (grey goat-feeder) and the Russian *Kozodoi*, which all translate as goat-milker or feeder. In fact, nightjars do indeed often come close to cattle, but this is because they feed on the insects that cattle attract. Presumably, farmers and cowherds misinterpreted what they saw, and assumed that the birds were taking milk from their stock. They must have thought this all the more if the animal had not been milked for some time and its teats were leaking.

Nightjars were quite common in the parish of Selborne in Hampshire, where the pioneering ornithologist Gilbert White (1720–93) was curate. He noted a widely held superstition that they could do great harm to calves by striking at them with their beaks and infecting the animals with a disease known locally as 'puckeridge', and wrote in his journal how unlikely this was to be true:

> The least observation and attention would convince men that these birds neither injure the goat-herd, nor the grazier; but

that they are perfectly harmless, and subsist alone, being night birds, on night-insects . . . nor does it anywise appear how they can, weak and unarmed as they seem, inflict any harm on kine [cattle], unless they possess the powers of animal magnetism, and can affect them by fluttering over them.

Gilbert White was right: the nightjar's beak is far too weak to penetrate the hide of a cow; and in reality the infection is caused by the warble fly – *Hypoderma bovis* – which lays its eggs beneath the skin on the animal's back. When the eggs hatch, the maggots burrow their way out through the hide, leaving the infection behind. The belief, however, was unshakeable, and so persistent that many country people called the nightjar bird itself a 'puckeridge'.

As if this unwholesome reputation wasn't bad enough, the people of Nidderdale in Yorkshire believed that the souls of unbaptized children took the form of nightjars, condemned to wander about the world eternally. They called the birds 'Gabbleratchets' or 'corpse hounds', the former being a variation of 'Gabriel's Hounds', who, it was said, could be heard baying at night. Quite how the churring call of the nightjar could possibly be confused with that of hounds, spectral or otherwise, is something of a mystery. Perhaps local people confused the call of the nightjar with that of an OWL.

In Greek mythology, the nightjar features in the story of Aigypios, a young man who fell in love with his friend's mother, the widow Timandra. Her son, Neophron, objected to the match, and in his bitterness he contrived to seduce Aigypios' mother, Boulis. But he didn't stop there. He eavesdropped on his mother and his friend, finding out when and where they had their romantic liaisons. By arranging with Boulis to meet in the darkened chamber where Timandra and Aigypios normally met, and then distracting his mother, he tricked Boulis and Aigypios into committing incest. When Boulis awoke to discover her son lying by her side, she took a dagger and blinded her son before plunging the blade into her breast. Zeus took pity on the victims of such a cruel stratagem and transformed Aigypios into a lammergeyer (a large Eurasian vulture), Neophron into an Egyptian vulture, Boulis into a seabird and Timandra into a nightjar.

Owl
(Tyto alba)

Mainly nocturnal and solitary birds, of which there are numerous species. The best known is probably the barn owl, which is white and brown and has a shrieking call. The tawny owl is more common and makes the more familiar 'too witt too whoo' calls.

Nocturnal birds tend, not surprisingly, to be the subject of deep fear and suspicion, and owls, with their silent flight and eerie calls, are no exception. Chaucer, for example, refers in his *Parlement of Fowles* to 'The owl eke [also], that of death the bode [omen] bringeth.' And Shakespeare similarly regarded it as the harbinger of misfortune and death. Its appearance in *Julius Caesar* is all the more sinister because it is not

seen at its appointed time but during the day. As Casca says (in Act I, Scene 3):

> And yesterday the bird of night did sit,
> Even at noonday, upon the market place,
> Hooting and shrieking.

In Shakespeare's time, people also believed that if an owl appeared at the birth of a child, this boded ill; hence, for example, the accusation King Henry VI levels at the wicked

Richard, Duke of Gloucester, in one of the final scenes of Shakespeare's *Henry VI, Part III*, 'The owl shrieked at thy birth, an evil sign.'

Nearly two thousand years earlier, owls had been greatly feared by the Romans, who, like so many other peoples over the centuries, believed the birds were the messengers of death. The poet Ovid wrote, 'Cowardly owl, an omen dreadful to mortals', and Pliny described it as: 'Bird of death and utterly abominable'. Three emperors, Augustus, Valentinian and Commodus Antonius, were thought to have died after an owl had alighted on the roof of their villas, and it is no doubt for this reason that any owl seen on the Capitol was treated extremely severely: it would be caught, then burnt, and its ashes would be thrown into the Tiber.

The Pima Indians of Arizona went even further in the link they made between owls and death, for they believed that owls actually contained the souls of the departed and that if an owl was heard hooting at the actual moment someone died it was a sign that it was waiting for that person's soul. Owl feathers were given to a dying person and were kept in a special long box ready for this purpose. If it so happened that a family did not already possess such feathers, then the medicine man, who always kept a stock of such things, would be fetched.

This link between owls and death also existed in ancient Egypt. When pharaohs decided they wished to be rid of a particular courtier or official, they would send him a picture of an owl. The message was unambiguous: the recipient was expected to take his own life. On a less sinister note, in hieroglyphics the sound 'm' was denoted by an owl, which, unusually for hieroglyphics, was drawn face out rather than in profile.

From the south of India comes a belief which is similar in some ways to rhymes in British folklore about MAGPIES, though here it is not a case of divining the future by counting how many birds could be seen, but by counting the number of cries that could be heard. If an owl screeched once it foretold death; twice, the success of some project; three times, a marriage; four, trouble; five, a journey; six, the arrival of visitors; seven, anxiety; eight, sudden death; and nine, a favourable event.

Many traditions record links between owls and children. In some cases, the link is part and parcel of the belief that owls portended the future; so, for example, in the South of France, it was thought that if an owl called from the chimney of a pregnant woman's house, then the baby would be a girl; in Jewish folklore, there was a fear that the calls of an owl could cause the death of infants, and a conviction that the way to prevent this happening was to pour water out into the courtyard so as to distract the bird. But in some traditions, there was an even more direct, physical link between the birds and the humans who feared them. The Berbers of North Africa, for instance, believed that owls, known as *sheerrees* from the sound they make, had two nipples on their breasts, like a woman, and that if they discovered a newborn child in an encampment, they would fly in silently at night and suckle the baby. One teat produced a special milk which would make the infant grow big and strong, but the other produced infected blood which would kill the child by morning. If a baby was found with oozing nostrils it was a sign that the *sheerree* was the culprit. Even today, in an effort to thwart the bird, some mothers of newborn babies cover their child's head when it's asleep. It's possible that the superstition arose from an attempt to account for what is known in western countries as cot death.

A parallel to this belief can be found in European folklore. The writer Titinius, who lived in the second century BC, advised that garlic should be placed on a baby to protect it from 'strix' (the Latin name for the screech owl), in case it 'should instil milk between their lips'. Centuries later, the medieval German philosopher Albertus Magnus referred to a very similar belief in his discussion of the 'bubo', or horned owl. He also called it an 'amma' – a name the owl had acquired, or so the Dominican friar Vincent de Beauvais claimed in his very popular encyclopaedia, because of its love for children (amma, he said, derived from the Latin verb *amare*, to love).

From these beliefs to a conviction that owls could play a significant role in witchcraft was a very small step indeed. The Romans held that Hecate, the goddess of the underworld and magic, had the owl as her ally, and since then many have come to believe that owls were actually the familiars of witches, carrying them on their evil expeditions on silent wings. Country people in Sweden argued that one should exercise a great deal of caution when talking about owls, for fear of angering them. Equally, should an owl be killed, there was a strong belief that its companions might come back to avenge its death. Not surprisingly, owls were thought to be a necessary ingredient in many witches' brews, too. The three witches in Shakespeare's *Macbeth* add an 'owlet's wing' to their magic potion, while Ben Jonson's *Masque of Queenes* makes reference to 'the screech owls' eggs and the feathers black'.

Proverbial birds

Many birds feature in proverbial sayings throughout the world. For example, in Holland people sometimes say, '*Wat baten kaars en bril, als den uil niet zienen wil?*', which literally means 'What use are candle and glasses if the owl does not want to see?' and is roughly equivalent to 'You can lead a horse to water, but you can't make him drink.' If you want to tell a Hungarian that money doesn't grow on trees, you might well say, '*Nem repül a sült galamb a szádba*', meaning 'Fried chicken doesn't fly into your mouth'; but if you're not great with money yourself you may well get the response '*Bagoly mondja a verébnek, hogy nagyfejű*', which means 'The owl calling the sparrow big-headed', in other words 'The pot calling the kettle black'. In Turkey, the problems with debating an issue for too long are summed up in the phrase '*Horozu çok olan köyün sabahı geç olur*', which means 'In a village with too many cockerels, morning will come late.' And in the Philippines, there is a proverb that warns against riches if all they bring is solitude: '*Aanhin mo ang palasyo, kung ang nakatira ay kuwago? Mabuti pa ang bahay kubo, ang nakatira ay tao*' or 'What good is a palace if it's inhabited by owls? Better a straw hut inhabited by people.'

That said, there is a counter-tradition to these negative and fearful beliefs. For many, the owl may have been a creature of the night, to be avoided and shunned. It may even have been regarded as a rather stupid bird (perhaps because it is confused and dazzled by daylight). However, to the ancient Greeks the owl was a symbol of sagacity, a bird sacred to Athene, the goddess of wisdom and victory, and frequently depicted on Greek coins. To catch sight of an owl was a good omen, as Aristophanes makes clear in his play *The Wasps*:

> Yet we drove their ranks before us, ere the fall of eventide,
> As we closed in, an owl flew o'er us and the gods were on
> our side.

The general Agathokles released a number of owls before the Greeks' victory over the Carthaginians in 310 BC, and when the birds flew among the troops and settled on their shields they served to boost morale considerably. In fact, 'There goes an owl' was a Greek saying that meant a victory was in prospect.

This rather more positive view of owls can be found in many aspects of folk medicine as well. Although they may have been used by witches for evil purposes, owls could be used by ordinary people to effect cures. In India, for example, it was thought that eating owls' eggs improved night vision. Local people would also place a few owls' feathers under the pillows of fractious babies to calm them. Conversely, the Cherokees of North America bathed their children's eyes with a liquid containing owls' feathers to help them stay awake at night. And people in Yorkshire believed that because owls can hoot without coming to any harm, a broth made from an owl would cure whooping cough. Meanwhile in Germany it was believed that placing the heart and right foot of an owl under the left armpit would ensure you'd never be bitten by a mad dog, while the Romans believed the ashes of an owl's feet to be a certain remedy against snake venom. Pliny also wrote that 'owlet' was a remedy for leech bites and insect stings.

Evidence of belief in the magic properties of the owl can be found all over the world. In Pennsylvania, an Amish belief was recorded in 1863 that claimed that placing the heart and right foot of a barn owl on a sleeping person would compel the sleeper to answer any question truthfully – this belief resembles one held by Albertus Magnus, probably quoting from Pliny, who observed that an owl's heart placed on the left breast of a sleeping woman would cause her to reveal her secrets. In Britain and Europe in the not-too-distant past, dead owls were nailed to barns as a protection against hail and lightning. Again, this is a belief with a long pedigree, being referred to by the Roman author Columella, who wrote a long tract on agriculture in the first century AD called *De Re Rustica*. It seems to be quite a widely held belief, too: in China, owls were known as 'thunder-averters', and special owl-like ornaments were fixed to the corners of roofs to protect houses against fire.

Among all these various folk remedies and charms, one of the longest standing – and certainly most bizarre – is that owls can prevent drunkenness. The ancient Greeks believed that any child who ate an owl's egg would never become an alcoholic, while in his 1643 work *Speculum mundi* (*The Mirror of the World*), John Swan wrote that owls' eggs broken in a cup would serve to cure a drunkard of his drunkenness. A more tangential link between owls and alcohol comes in the first-century AD medical treatise called *Cyranides*, which, in addition to prescribing a soup made from an owl's egg and eaten at the

~~~~~~

time of the waning moon as a cure for epilepsy, also recommended salted owl as good for gout. Since excessive consumption of alcohol was thought to cause gout, this proposed cure seems to form part of a wider pattern of beliefs.

No description of owls in folklore would be complete without an account of the legend that lies behind the remark 'They say the owl was a baker's daughter' that Ophelia makes in Shakespeare's *Hamlet* shortly before her suicide. The legend tells how Jesus went into a baker's shop for something to eat. The baker put some dough into the oven to make a cake, but his daughter thought he was being too generous, so she took the dough out of the oven and halved it. When the cake was done it turned out to be enormous and the daughter cried, 'Hoo! hoo! hoo!' in surprise. She was immediately turned into an owl by Jesus as a punishment for her miserliness. Similar stories are told about LAPWINGS and WOODPECKERS.

Peacock
(Pavo cristatus)

The male bird has iridescent blue-green plumage and a head crest, and the female is brown and without long tail feathers. The mating display, where the male fans out its feathers and utters distinctive calls to attract the female, is spectacular.

Despite the fact that its native home is in Asia, the peacock is a familiar bird throughout much of the world, having been

introduced to Europe via ancient Greece. Its beauty and haughty demeanour can hardly fail to catch the eye; appropriately enough, in heraldry, a peacock displaying its tail feathers is described as being 'in his pride'. Given its flamboyance, it's easy to understand how the birds have tended to become status symbols, familiar sights in the grounds of many palaces and stately homes.

To the ancient Greeks, the peacock was held to be sacred to Hera, who was married to Zeus, king of the gods. Zeus was extremely promiscuous (see, for example, the CUCKOO and SWAN for further stories about him) and quite unable to resist a pretty woman, be she goddess or human. At one time, he was greatly attracted to a young woman called Io, so much so, in fact, that Hera became highly suspicious. In an attempt to allay her jealousy, Zeus turned the unfortunate Io into a heifer (how the once-beautiful Io felt about this transformation we are not told). Hera, however, was not at all mollified by this gesture, and she commanded her servant Argus, who had one hundred eyes, to keep a close watch on the situation. Zeus retaliated by ordering his messenger, Hermes (god of travellers), to lull Argus to sleep with beautiful music and then kill him. Greatly distressed by this, Hera took some of Argus' eyes and placed them on the tail of her favourite bird in commemoration of her faithful servant.

Even though peacocks are famous for their beauty, a good deal of negative superstition persists to this day regarding the possession and use of peacock feathers. Many actors, for instance, believe that to have peacock feathers on the stage will bring disaster to a play. In some places, it was formerly thought that peacock feathers in a house would either result in any spinster who lived there remaining unmarried or in general bad luck. Such ideas appear to have their root in the concept of the evil eye – the belief that some individuals had the power to harm or even kill with a glance. That said, it does seem to be the case that this is a very late superstition – probably arising at some point in the mid nineteenth century. Certainly, many people in the West were and are happy to wear peacock feathers, while in China, for example, peacock feathers were worn regularly at official functions. During the Tang dynasty (AD 618–907), many districts paid their tributes to the emperor with peacock feathers. He, in turn, awarded them to officials, both civil and military, for their good conduct and long service. The feathers were graded according to the services being recognized, and were classified as 'one-eyed', 'two-eyed' and 'three-eyed', 'flower' and 'green' feathers.

In their lands of origin – the East, and India in particular – peacocks are regarded very affectionately, their loud screeches being regarded as a useful warning of approaching predators, such as tigers or leopards, or of more general danger. One legend tells how a general of the Chinese Qin dynasty, defeated in battle, took refuge in a forest in which there were known to be a great number of peacocks. When his pursuing enemies finally reached the forest, all was quiet, so they assumed that he could not have hidden there; if he had, the peacocks would surely have betrayed him. In time, the defeated general became a king, and to honour the peacocks that had protected him he decreed that in future their feathers should be awarded as a mark of bravery in battle.

One rather strange belief is that the peacock is ashamed of its large black feet. Robert Chester in *Love's Martyr* (1601), for example, refers to:

> The proud sun-loving peacock with his feathers
> Walks all alone, thinking himself a king
> But when he lookes downe to his base blacke feete
> He droops, and is ashamed of things unmete.

Similarly, the medieval Persian poet Azz'Eddin Elmocadessi describes:

> The peacock wedded to the world
> Of all her gorgeous plumage vain
> With glowing banners wide unfurled
> Sweeps slowly by in proud disdain.
> But in her heart a torment lies
> That dims the brightness of her eyes
> She turns away her glance – but no
> Her hideous feet appear below.

Pelican
(Pelecanus onocrotalus)

A waterbird with a distinctive pouch under its beak, it can grow to have a wingspan of three metres. Pelicans are social birds, nesting and often hunting in groups – they are monogamous during the breeding season but afterwards move on to find a new mate.

The strange behaviour and idiosyncratic appearance of pelicans have fascinated and beguiled man through the centuries. To the Seri, an indigenous group of people living in the Mexican state of Sonora, the pelican represented the creator of the world: a god who raised the land from beneath the waters that once covered all the earth. Not only was this pelican revered as their creator but, additionally, it was credited with the possession of

a beautiful singing voice. This seems, it has to be said, a rather strange belief, given that the bird's 'song' consists mainly of a series of croaks and grunts.

In Europe in the Middle Ages, the pelican had the reputation for being a truly pious bird and so became a symbol of Jesus, associated particularly with the Eucharist and the Passion of Christ. This connection arose because it was widely believed that the pelican possessed a special ability to restore its offspring to life by feeding them with its own blood, echoing Jesus's words at the Last Supper, 'this is my blood of the new testament, which is shed for many for the remission of sins.' The fourth-century scholar Jerome, for instance, states, 'As the pelican's young killed by serpents were revived by their mother's blood, so was the salvation by Christ towards those dead in sin.' This ability to revive its young is, however, only part of the story, even though it's the best-known part. Originally, it was thought that the reason the young died in the first place was because the male pelican, irritated at the sight of his growing brood, actually took it upon himself to kill them. Overcome by remorse, he then gave them his own blood to revive them. This may seem a rather strange idea, but it's almost certainly based on first-hand observation, though it is a case of misinterpreted observation. Parent pelicans feed their young macerated food from the large pouch under their bill. Early observers clearly thought that it was blood that was being transferred.

Not even faulty observation can quite explain Aristotle's extraordinary description of the pelican's method of feeding:

> Pelicans living by rivers swallow big smooth shells. After cooking them in its pouch in front of its stomach they vomit them up, so that when they are open they can pick out the flesh and eat it.

Dionysius of Halicarnassus, writing in the first century BC, also had some very strange theories about the bird's feeding habits. Like Aristotle, he, too, believed in the cooked shellfish story, but he also added:

> They have very long necks and are as voracious as shearwaters ... They do not dive completely under the water but dip their necks, which are six feet long; keeping their body above the

water, they take every fish that they find. In front they have a kind of pouch into which they put all their food, refraining neither from cockles or hard mussels, but gulping everything down, shell and all. When the creatures are dead they vomit up the mouthful, eat the flesh and expel the shells.

Finally, a peculiar story, recorded by Horapollo in the fourth century AD, tells how people set about capturing pelicans:

Although the pelican is capable of laying its eggs in quite inaccessible places it does nothing of the kind. Instead it digs a hole in the ground and deposits its offspring in it. Seeing what the bird is up to the catchers surround the spot with dried ox dung and set fire to it. When the pelican sees the smoke its great efforts to extinguish the fire by flapping its wings only make the fire worse and it sets fire to itself by mistake.

Quail
(Coturnix coturnix)

Small migrant game birds. Their bodies are plump and their wings long and pointed. They eat seeds and insects and nest on the ground. The quail is rarely seen, but its 'quick wi wick' call is often heard. In Britain, the bird arrives late in April or early May and stays until late summer.

During their wanderings in the desert following their flight from Egypt, the Israelites begged God for meat to supplement their endless diet of manna. In response, God sent them great flocks of quail, which they enthusiastically killed and ate. Soon after, as the Bible records, 'The Lord smote them with a very great plague' (Numbers 2). It is possible to speculate that this sudden onset of illness arose from salmonella poisoning, caused by eating flesh that had become infected in the hot weather. But it's interesting to note that quail, long esteemed by people for its flesh and eggs, also once had a reputation for being unwholesome. The Roman writer Pliny the Elder, for example, stated that:

> The flesh of the quail, though in high esteem in our own days, was supposed by ancient authors to be very heating and unwholesome, from the birds' fondness for poisonous plants.

To balance this, though, was a belief that quail had powerful medicinal qualities. Some people thought the flesh was good for kidney problems; others maintained that eating its brain was held to be a certain cure for epilepsy (though, just to make matters confusing, the claim was also sometimes made that since the bird had a particular fondness for the seed of hellebore plants, eating it, far from curing epilepsy, would actually cause the condition).

A number of stories have been told about the migrations of quails. The eighteenth-century French naturalist Count Georges Buffon, for example, recorded a very old belief that when quails needed to elect a king to lead them on their long flight they chose a corncrake. The same idea is found in Aristotle's writings, though he believed that the leader was not a corncrake but an OWL. This inevitably raises the question why quails would want to go to the lengths of choosing a leader from another species in the first place. The answer tradition-ally supplied was that the quails knew that the first bird to arrive on land after an arduous sea crossing would be so exhausted that it could easily fall prey to a predator such as a falcon, so they hit on the idea of choosing an outsider as leader. The story reflects well on the perceived cunning of quails, if not, perhaps, on their honesty.

The Greek writer Dionysius of Halicarnassus asserted that when the birds migrated at night, they would carry three stones

A bird in the hand is worth two in the bush

This well-known proverb is found in a similar form in many different languages. Here are just a few examples:

- Czech: *Lepší vrabec v hrsti než holub na střeše* (Better a sparrow in the hand than a pigeon on the roof)
- Finnish: *Parempi pyy pivossa, kuin kymmenen oksalla* (Better one hazel grouse in the bag than ten on the branch)
- Indonesian: *Lebih baik satu burung ditangan dari pada sepuluh burung dipohon* (Better one bird in the hand than ten birds on the tree)
- Italian: *É meglio oggi l'uovo, che domani la gallina* (Better the egg today than the hen tomorrow)
- Russian: *Ne suli ʒhuravlya v nebe, a day sinitsu v ruki* (Don't promise the crane in the sky, but give the titmouse in your hand)

in their beaks, which they would drop at intervals so that they could gauge by the sounds made by the falling stones whether they were flying over land or sea. He also stated that they were so frightened of the sea that they closed their eyes when crossing it. This was supposed to account for the birds' constant tendency to collide with ships' sails and rigging.

A further story about quails and the sea, which bears a strong resemblance to the myth of the barnacle GOOSE, is recounted in *The Magic of Kirani, King of Persia*, which was translated into English and published in 1685:

A quail is a bird known to all, yet its nature is not easily known for there is one thing concerning this unknown. For, when there are great storms upon the coasts of the Libya deserts, the sea casts up great tunas on the shore, and these breed worms for fourteen days and grow to be as big as flies, then locusts, which be augmented in bigness become birds called quails.

On land, the quail lives in deep grass and growing crops, so it is more often heard than seen. As a result, stories arose in a number of places about the significance of its call. In Swabia, peasants once believed that the number of times the birds called signified the price their corn would fetch at harvest time. Similar beliefs were also to be found in central and western France, Switzerland and in Tuscany. In the Austrian Tyrol, a young bachelor would count the first calls of the quail in spring carefully, as these denoted the number of years he would remain unmarried.

Among the stranger reaches of quail lore is the suggestion that if the eyes of a quail are dissolved in a little water for seven days, then mixed with oil and set alight in a candle or on a rag, anyone nearby will take on the appearance of a devil on fire. This potion can also be used for even more magical purposes. By combining a few drops with a sardonyx stone that has been engraved with a quail and a sea tench, you can make a ring that will turn its wearer invisible.

Raven
(Corvus corax)

A very large, heavy-looking member of the crow family that prefers wild hills and mountains and eats a large variety of prey, alive and dead. In the past it was associated with scavenging on battle-fields, hence its generally bad reputation. It is extremely intelligent, a good mimic and agile in flight.

Given how distinctive ravens are, it is scarcely surprising that they have inspired such a body of folklore and legend. What is surprising, though, is that despite their black plumage, eerie call and habit – at least, in the past – of frequenting battlefields and feeding off the dead, their reputation has not been an entirely negative one.

As portents or omens, for example, they can augur favourable as well as unfavourable outcomes. It was widely believed that

a raven seen at the start of important activities such as hunting or fishing foretold good fortune. Indeed, in the Highlands of Scotland it was extremely encouraging to hear one croak if you were setting out deer-stalking. In seventeenth-century Ireland, seeing a raven with white on its wing (a rather unlikely event) flying on one's right-hand side and croaking at the same time was an infallible sign of good fortune.

That said, many of the superstitions about ravens are, inevitably, negative ones. Typical of these is the Andalusian belief that if a raven croaks over a house an unlucky day will result; if it croaks three times a death will follow; and if it perches somewhere high up and turns and croaks repeatedly, a corpse will come from that direction. In Act II of Christopher Marlowe's *The Jew of Malta*, the raven is unambiguously an evil omen:

> . . . the sad presaging raven, that tolls
> The sick man's passport in her hollow beak,
> And in the shadow of the silent night
> Doth shake contagion from her sable wings.

While in Act I, Scene 5 of Shakespeare's *Macbeth*, Lady Macbeth welcomes the arrival of Duncan – the man she wants her husband to kill – with the chilling words:

> The raven himself is hoarse
> That croaks the fatal entrance of Duncan
> Under my battlements.

Some fifteen hundred years earlier, the Roman statesman Cicero was said to have been warned of his own death by fluttering ravens and then awakened by a raven pulling at his bedclothes on the day he was murdered.

In parts of Germany it was thought that ravens contained the souls of the damned and even, at times, the soul of the devil himself, while in the Languedoc region of France it was wicked priests whose souls were said to inhabit ravens; wicked nuns had to content themselves with ending up inside crows. In Sweden it was the souls of murdered people who had not received a proper Christian burial that dwelled inside the birds.

One of the best-known beliefs about ravens is the supposedly centuries-old tradition that, should they forsake the Tower of London, Britain's downfall will swiftly follow. Sadly, recent research by Dr Geoff Parnell, the official Tower of London historian, suggests that this tradition is in fact a Victorian invention. Nevertheless, it is a myth that has clearly caught the public imagination, and twentieth-century keepers of the Tower have gone to great lengths to keep ravens in the grounds. During the Second World War, the birds were all killed in bombing raids, but new ones were brought in for the Tower's reopening in 1946. Today, the ravens at the Tower are tamed and pinioned to prevent them escaping.

In addition to being regarded as omens, whether good or bad, ravens also took the role of messengers in many legends. In Tibet it was thought that they acted on behalf of a supreme being, and the Chinese believed that it was a raven that caused a storm to blow through the forests to warn the inhabitants when the gods were about to pass. The twentieth-century ornithologist Edward A. Armstrong conjectured that the raven was once a god in some distant and past religion, and that in the course of time the bird had been either deposed or demoted, but retained its privileged position as messenger or ambassador to its successors. Greek mythology echoes Eastern religions by portraying the raven as a messenger to the gods in some stories. For example, it was a raven who came to tell Apollo (the god of healing and medicine) that his lover Koronis had been unfaithful. Incensed, Apollo sent his sister Artemis to kill the girl.

In the world of the Vikings, the raven was worshipped and revered. It was the symbol of the chief of the gods, Odin, and all his followers carried an image of the bird on their shields and banners. The *Landeyda* (land ravager) was a famous war banner that bore the emblem of a raven and was reputed to have been woven in one day by the granddaughter of Sigurd, a hero of Norse mythology who had the power to understand the language of the birds. Odin himself owned two ravens: Hugin (thought) and Munin (memory). Since it was widely believed that ravens had the power of human speech and could understand what they heard, Hugin and Munin were thought to fly all over the world every day, returning to Odin's shoulder to tell him all they had seen and heard. This myth is echoed in the Irish phrase 'raven's knowledge', which applies to anyone who appears to see and know all.

The Vikings' faith in the bird's powers of observation stretched to the belief that it actually had the power to anticipate future slaughter and would, as a consequence, follow armies in order to benefit from the feasts to come. One Viking song asks:

> How is it with you ravens, whence are you come
> With gory beak at the dawning of the day?
> You lodged last night I ween [suppose]
> Where you knew the corpses were lying.

In other mythological traditions, the raven was connected with the creation of the world and with the flood that many people thought had once inundated the earth. The Koyukon people, hunters living on the Koyukuk river in Alaska, believed that the great raven Dot-son-paa made the world, and that when the great flood came he placed two of every animal, bird and insect upon a raft so that they would survive. To this day, the Koyukon people treat all wildlife with the courtesy that they accord to human beings, but make a special point of showing particular respect to the raven. The Koyukon's near neighbours, the Tlingit tribe, believed that the raven was the mythical ancestor of their race and performed many wonderful deeds at the beginning of the world. Among these was deciding what particular task each bird should perform, where they should live and what colour their plumage was to be. One story relates that the raven decreed that the (American) ROBIN should give pleasure to man through its beauty, and the hummingbird through its song; another tells how he commanded all the birds to dress differently so that they would be able to recognize each other – the blue jay, for example, was told to pile its hair high and tie it with a string. As for himself, the magical raven could transform himself into whatever shape he chose and could remove his feathers like a coat. As a spirit of creation he had no beginning and no end.

As with several other black-plumaged birds (see, for example, the BLACKBIRD), there was a widespread belief that the raven had originally been white, but had been turned black as a punishment for some evil deed. One legend, well known in the Austrian Tyrol, related how, as a child, Jesus had wished to drink from a stream whose waters had been fouled by several ravens; as a punishment, he turned their plumage black. In Greenland, the story was that the raven once made a special summer coat for the snowy OWL, and in return the owl made the raven a white suit and a pair of whalebone boots. While his suit was being fitted, the raven kept fidgeting and wriggling about, and this made it difficult for the owl to get the right fit. Finally, the owl became so cross with the raven that he warned him that he would pour lamp oil on him if he didn't keep still. The raven persisted in hopping about, so the owl carried out his threat and the raven has remained black ever since. For their part, the Cherokee Indians believed that it was ash that had turned the raven's feathers black. They thought that the raven had tried to bring fire to the world from a hollow tree which had been set alight by a bolt of lightning from the thunder god and that the bird had become blackened by smoke and soot in the attempt.

In common with the SWALLOW, the EAGLE and the toad, the raven was thought in some European traditions to possess a magical stone that could act as a valuable talisman in the treatment of a variety of human conditions. There were reputed to be three kinds of stone: the 'release' stone, the 'invisibility' stone and the 'life' stone. To obtain the first, all you had to do was to muzzle some nestlings' beaks on St Vitus' Day (15 June), wait for the henbird to discover what had happened, watch as she flew away to collect the magic stone that would set the chicks free, and then steal the stone before the raven flew away again. This 'release' stone was believed to be a valuable aid in childbirth. The second stone was obtained by boiling a raven's egg and then replacing it in the nest for the henbird to 'incubate'. If it was removed before the henbird deserted the nest, the egg would be found to contain a stone that, if placed beneath the right armpit, would make you invisible. The third and most powerful kind of raven stone was extremely difficult to acquire. The henbird had to be more than one hundred years old and her young less than six weeks. All the young would have to be killed in the nest except for one male whose bill would be propped open in readiness for the magic red stone which the hen would bring to it once she had seen what had happened to her other chicks. If you could seize the stone before the male chick got it, and then placed it under the left armpit, you would evoke powerful magic that could prolong life and even bring the dead back to life.

Perhaps the most celebrated of all ravens was one that lived during the reign of the emperor Tiberius (AD 14–37). This bird had made its home at a cobbler's shop near the Temple of Castor and every morning flew off to find the same spot near the forum where it greeted Tiberius and, later, the popular Roman general Germanicus, calling them by name and greeting other passers-by. This continued for a number of years, until a neighbouring shopkeeper became so jealous of the celebrity enjoyed both by the raven and by the cobbler's shop where it nested that he killed the bird. A storm of fury ensued, the offending shopkeeper was driven out of the district and later murdered, and huge crowds turned out to attend the raven's funeral. The corpse was placed upon a bier which was heaped with wreaths and carried by two slaves, while a piper led the way to a funeral pyre that had been specially built near the Appian Way. 'No such crowds', Pliny recorded, 'had ever escorted the funeral of anyone out of the whole number of Rome's distinguished men.'

Robin
(Erithacus rubecula)

A plump, perky bird, mostly olive-brown but with a bright orange forehead, breast and throat. Males and females look identical. Despite its sweet appearance, the bird is fiercely territorial and aggressive towards other robins. It sings all year round and will sing at night next to street lights. In 1966, it became Britain's national bird following a popularity poll.

Such is the fondness felt for robins that there are many taboos against killing or harming one. In Norse mythology it was believed that the robin was sacred to Thor, the god of lightning, and that if the bird or its nest was wantonly destroyed, whoever was responsible would be annihilated by lightning or fire. Similarly, in Devon, people thought that the destroyer of a robin's nest would come to no good, while the following traditional rhyme from Essex includes the robin in a whole list of birds that should be left well alone:

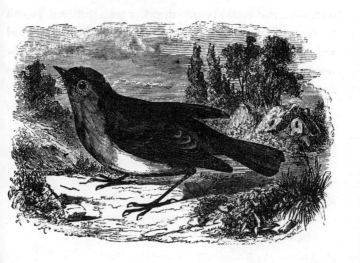

The robin and the redbreast
The robin and the wren,
If ye take out of the nest
Ye'll never thrive again.
The robin and the redbreast
The martin and the swallow,
If you touch one of their eggs
Bad luck is sure to follow.

Such beliefs weren't restricted to England. In the Austrian Tyrol, for example, it was thought that anyone who harmed a robin or its nest would suffer epileptic fits – a belief that has resonances with the Suffolk saying that if a robin dies in your hand it will shake for evermore. Nor were humans thought to be the only ones who would be punished if a robin suffered. People in Hertfordshire argued that any cat that killed a robin would be fated to lose a limb. Given the number of robins killed by cats and the conspicuous lack of cats with missing legs, this does seem a rather perverse view.

Christian tradition also accords the robin an honourable place in the hierarchy of birds. One widespread story tells how the robin shared in Jesus' agony on the Cross, and, as a result, carries a drop of God's blood in its veins to this day. Consequently, so the argument went, it wasn't merely bad luck to harm such a bird, it was also a sin – a sentiment recorded in 'The Redbreast, a Bretton Legend' by the nineteenth-century English writer John Hoskyns-Abrahall:

> Since then no wanton boy disturbs her nest:
> Weasel nor wild cat with her young molest,
> All sacred deem the bird of ruddy breast.

Various versions exist of the story of the robin's role in the Crucifixion, two of the most noteworthy coming from Brittany. The first tells how the robin tried to remove a thorn from Jesus' crown of thorns as he carried his cross to Calgary, piercing its own breast in the process and becoming covered in blood. It then kept the stain as a mark of its piety. The second version tells how two birds were perched on the Cross while Jesus was being crucified. One was the MAGPIE, who at that time was the most colourful of all the birds, with a tuft of feathers on his head and a tail to rival the PEACOCK. True to its wicked nature, it insulted the dying Jesus. The other bird was a robin, small and drab. It flew to Jesus with comforting chirps, wiped away his tears with its wings and attempted to remove the thorns from his crown. As it did so, a drop of Jesus' blood fell on to its breast, turning its dull-brown plumage bright red. Jesus blessed the bird, proclaiming that from then on it would be a bearer of good tidings, with happiness and joy following wherever it went. He also decreed that henceforth its eggs would be as blue as the heavens. The magpie he cursed to be sad and sombre, to live a hard life and to have a nest that would always be open to storms.

A legend from modern Greece tells how, as a child, Jesus would feed the robins outside his parents' home. A close bond was thus formed, and, many years later, the robin refused to leave Jesus' tomb until he had risen from the dead. It then sang with the angels as Jesus ascended to heaven.

The robin is also credited with having helped the Virgin Mary. One day, a piece of straw was blown into her eye, and a robin, who was perched nearby, immediately flew off to seek help from the SWALLOW and also to collect some pure water in its bill. This it carefully dropped into her eye while the swallow drew one of its long tail feathers under her eyelid and gently removed the piece of straw.

Another legend with a religious theme connects the robin with the sixth-century saint Kentigern (also known as St Mungo). As a young monk, St Kentigern trained in Scotland under St Serf, who had a pet robin that would feed out of his hand and sit on his shoulder and twitter while the psalms were being sung. St Kentigern was a favourite of St Serf, and this provoked a lot of jealousy among the other young men at the seminary.

To spite Kentigern, they killed the robin and placed the blame for the deed on him. He, however, prayed over the corpse, and the bird revived so completely that it was able to greet St Serf when he returned from his devotions.

An old legend from Brittany records how a party of monks who had come to convert the pagan inhabitants there found life to be very precarious; they had no seeds to plant, and thus no possibility of raising any crops. One day, they saw a robin perched upon a cross they had erected, and hanging from the bird's bill was an ear of corn. The grateful monks collected it, planted the seeds, and after their first harvest replanted all they had grown. Ultimately, they not only had enough for their own needs, but were able to supply the whole district. As recently as the nineteenth century, local people would say that corn came to their country from the redbreast's one ear.

One of the most famous of all stories to do with robins is that of the 'Babes in the Wood', which tells how two children, abandoned by their wicked uncle in Wayland Wood in Norfolk, starved to death and were covered with leaves by a merciful robin. The story achieved widespread popularity when it was turned into a play in the nineteenth century, but it actually has its roots in sixteenth-century folklore and a widely held belief that robins would piously cover up any human corpses they encountered. In his *Most Famous History of the Seven Champions of Christendom*, published in 1596, the romance writer Richard Johnson, for example, mentions that murder victims were covered with moss and leaves by robins, while the Jacobean playwright John Webster writes in *The White Devil* (Act V, Scene 1):

> Call for the robin red-breast and the wren,
> Since o'er shady groves they hover,
> And with leaves and flowers do cover
> The friendless bodies of unburied men.

The same idea is to be found in the long poem *The Owl* (1604) by the English poet Michael Drayton, which tells how:

> Covering with moss the dead's unclosed eye,
> The little redbreast teacheth charitie.

And it is to be found, too, in *Cornucopia* by the great eighteenth-century writer and lexicographer Samuel Johnson:

> The robin redbreast, if he find a man or woman dead will cover his face with moss, and some think that if the body should remain unburied he will cover the whole body.

Interestingly, robins are often mentioned as having appeared at executions and funerals. At the lying in state of Queen Mary II in 1695 in Westminster Abbey, for example, one, known as 'The Westminster Wonder', perched on the queen's catafalque. Stories from Lorraine and parts of Germany also record the presence of robins at funerals, while in Brittany it was said that the robin would continue to sing his sad little song over the dead and refuse to leave until the body was buried. The explanation given for this was that the robin was performing this rite on behalf of a pagan god (usually Thor), who was the bird's protector.

Alongside the tradition associating the robin's red breast with Jesus' crucifixion is one that links it with fire. In Guernsey it was thought that the robin brought fire to the island from the mainland and that while flying across the water with it, its feathers became singed. Perhaps by way of compensation, it also managed to acquire the ability to speak Latin in the course of its journey. A French variation of this story maintains that it was the WREN that brought the fire, that in doing so all its feathers got burned away, and that the concerned robin then stood too close to the still-smouldering wren, scorching itself in the process.

In a story from the north of England, the fire that burned the robin's breast emanated from hell, where the robin would travel, carrying a drop of water in its beak, to alleviate the suffering of those incarcerated there. As the nineteenth-century American poet John Greenleaf Whittier wrote in 'The Robin':

> He brings cool dew in his little bill,
> And lets it fall on the souls of sin,
> You can see the mark on his red breast still
> Of fires that scorch as he drops it in.

Rook
(Corvus frugilegus)

Large black crows with a whitish-grey face and much smaller than ravens. Gregarious both in nesting and feeding, very vocal around their nests and in flight, they seem to delight in the gusty winds of autumn.

Rather like RAVENS, rooks were formerly thought to play an important role in foretelling the future. If a rookery was built close to a house, it was considered to be lucky, perhaps because it was believed that rooks kept away the crows that were believed to eat young chickens. In England, in places as far apart as Cornwall and Northumberland, rooks were believed to abandon

both their nests and their young prior to the departure or death of one of the family on whose land their rookery stood. In the nineteenth century, for example, it was reported that following the suicide of a Mr Graves from Linwood Grange in Rutland, a whole colony of rooks departed en masse when the hearse appeared, and only a very few ever returned, despite the fact that most had young in the nest. At Looe in Cornwall, it was similarly held that rooks would desert an estate on the death of the owner if there was no heir to inherit. At Chipcase in Northumberland, the rooks were reported to have abandoned their colony on the departure of the Reed family, the owners of the estate.

In Shropshire, it was believed that rooks never carried sticks to their nests on Sundays or Ascension Day, but simply sat quietly on the trees and did no work; another belief was that should a person not take the trouble to wear new clothes on Easter Day, the rooks would defecate on the old ones. This reputation for piety may well have stemmed from an old belief that rooks escorted the souls of the righteous to heaven, a belief hinted at in the opening line of William Butler Yeats' poem 'The Cold Heaven' (1916): 'Suddenly I saw the cold and rook-delighting Heaven'. As a further instance of the rook's sense of propriety it was said in Landebia in Brittany that because the widows of the village had a tradition of not remarrying, the rooks showed their respect by never eating the grain in that village but only corn planted in the neighbouring fields.

Bird droppings

Many people still believe that being hit by a bird dropping, though annoying, brings good luck. But there is a contradictory, and perhaps older, superstition that suggests that being hit by a bird dropping is a punishment for not wearing new clothes at Easter or Whitsun. Rooks, having the reputation of being particularly pious birds, were thought to play judge, jury and executioner in these cases.

Much of the lore concerning rooks relates to their ability to forecast changes in the weather. In Devon, it was assumed that should the birds stay in the vicinity of their nests in the middle of the day, or return to the rookery early, then rain would be near, but if they flew far away, then fine weather would be sure to follow. In Yorkshire, the saying went that if the rooks congregated on dead branches of trees, rain would come before nightfall, but if they perched on live branches it would be fine and dry.

The less attractive features of the rook – in particular, its cunning and predatory nature – have made their effect felt on the English language. The verb 'to rook' means to cheat someone, while a 'rookery' in nineteenth-century London was one of several notorious slums in the East End that were infested with criminals. Here the allusion is not only to the rook's dishonest nature but to the way that rooks build their nests very close together, just as the slums crowded in on each other.

The Latin name for the rook, *frugilegus*, meaning 'acquisitive', further points up the bird's predatory nature, typified by the way in which birds in a rookery will steal twigs from their neighbours' nests, given half a chance. So disliked were they in Ireland, in fact, that they even figured in an oath, 'The curse of the crows on you'.

Stonechat
(Saxicola torquata)

Rather plump, bright little bird. The male has an orange breast, a black head, white around his neck and a white flash on his wings. The female has the same orange breast but is otherwise brown. The bird constantly flicks its tail when sitting on low bushes and its call sounds like two stones being knocked together (hence the name).

In parts of Scotland, especially on the Isle of Harris in the Hebrides, the stonechat and the frog were thought to be strange, outlandish creatures that were closely associated in some mysterious way. Some believed that the bird nested among the stones on the shore of lochs and streams, and that when it left its nest, frogs would take its place and incubate its eggs for it. Others suggested that should a frog incubate the eggs of any bird, then regardless of the species of the parent birds, the nestlings would hatch as stonechats; hence, presumably, the local expression that 'The stone-chatterer is the frog's grandchild.'

Such a casual attitude to its offspring did not win the stonechat the best of reputations, and it seems to have been regarded as

an unlucky bird. The three cold days that April is often said to have borrowed from March are still known on Harris as 'The three days of punishment of the stone-chatterer'. Elsewhere in the Hebrides, the bird's reputation was even worse, although, paradoxically, it was also one of the three 'sacred' birds that were to be respected and never killed – the other two were the corncrake and the CUCKOO. It could be that people were worried about where the birds went when they migrated in the autumn. One theory was that they went to visit the 'little people', another that they were messengers from another world. All bear witness to the sense of unease that the islanders felt.

Like various other species of birds, stonechats were thought to be useful when it came to the art of telling the future. The nineteenth-century folklorist Alexander Carmichael, for instance, noted that it was considered to be a lucky omen if the first stonechat of the year was sighted on grass, but unlucky if it was seen on a rock or the road. In some parts of Britain, it was also thought to be able to forecast the weather. In Suffolk, where the stonechat is known as the whin chuck, it was believed that when the bird perched on the very top of a gorse bush, it foretold rainy weather. Presumably not many stonechats have been noted doing this in Suffolk, as the county is one of the driest in Britain.

Stork
(Ciconia ciconia)

Up to three feet and three inches (one metre) tall and with a six-and-a-half-foot (two-metre) wingspan, this long-legged bird has a long neck and is completely white apart from its bright red bill and legs and black wing feathers. It flies in a distinctive manner with its neck and legs extended, and winters in Africa before migrating to southern Europe for the spring.

The idea, familiar from countless greetings cards, that babies are brought by storks is also an astonishingly ubiquitous one,

being found not only in European culture but among, for example, the Sioux Indians. Quite how it arose is not clear. It may have something to do with the fact that the great flocks of storks that fly north from Africa at the beginning of each spring created an association in many people's minds with fertility. At a more practical level, it may be that the stork's considerable size made the idea that it could carry a newly born human from a secret spring and lay it in its mother's lap at least feasible. Whatever the truth of the matter, the link between this bird and humans has remained deeply embedded in popular consciousness.

Far less familiar today is the view that the stork's caring nature extends to its own parents as well. This, however, was once a popularly held belief. Indeed, in ancient Rome there was even a law requiring citizens to care for their elderly relatives that was known as the *Lex Ciconia*, or stork law. The idea seems to go hand in hand with a parallel belief in some places that storks lived to a ripe old age. The ancient Chinese attributed this longevity to the role that storks were believed to perform in carrying human souls, particularly those of brave soldiers, up to heaven.

But although storks were thought to be caring towards their parents and human babies, towards their own young it was quite a different matter. Here, they had a reputation for strictness, and for pecking vigorously, even to the point of making their young bleed. Fortunately, though, they had the extraordinary ability to heal any wounds they inflicted, as the sixteenth-century English writer John Lyly describes in his book *Euphues*: 'Ladies use their lovers as the stork doth her young ones who pecketh them till they bleed with her bill, and then healeth them with her tongue.' It is perhaps for this reason that the reddish-pink marks on the eyelids of newborn children are sometimes known as stork bites.

Most of the traditions concerning the stork are tied up with aspects of family life, but the bird was also thought in some places to be a lucky token. For example, in Greece it was believed that if a woman befriended a stork, the bird would one day return and lay a jewel at her feet as a token of affection. Similarly, in Central Europe it was thought that should a farmer provide a safe nesting place on his house or barn, the storks would reward him with a feather at the end of the first year, an egg after the second year and a young bird after the third.

~~~~~~

This belief that a stork's nest brought good luck encouraged many farmers to place a cartwheel on their roofs to make a platform on which the bird could build its nest. Conversely, it was thought that if the stork were to leave the farm, bad luck would certainly follow.

There are various stories as to how the bird got its name. One Swedish legend tells how, as Jesus hung dying from the Cross, a stork flew around him crying, 'Styrka, styrka' ('Strengthen, strengthen'). More prosaically, it has been suggested that the word 'stork' is related to the Old English word *stearc*, meaning 'stiff', a reflection of the bird's rigid posture. Some have even suggested that it ultimately derives from the Greek word *torgos*, meaning 'vulture'.

In heraldry, the stork represents filial duty and gratitude. It is also sometimes shown gorging on or holding a snake in its bill – a reference to the belief that storks and snakes were deadly enemies.

Swallow
(Hirundo rustica)

An agile bird that eats insects on the wing. Its plumage is dark metallic blue above and white below with a chestnut-red throat and forehead. It has long wings and a deeply forked tail.

The swallow is almost universally regarded as the herald of spring. The ancient Greeks even held a festival to honour its

arrival on the island of Rhodes during which children would
welcome the bird with a song:

> He comes, he comes, who loves to hear
> Soft sunny hours and seasons fair
> The swallow hither comes for rest
> His sable wing and snowy breast.

The arrival of the first swallows continued to be celebrated in
parts of Greece until the beginning of the twentieth century.
In some districts, swallows were captured and smeared with oil
before being released to continue their journey in order to

remove ill luck from the house. In Russia, meanwhile, numerous songs were composed to celebrate their return after the long dark winter, and in Westphalia farmers and their families would wait at their gates to welcome the birds and throw open the barn doors to allow them to enter. Further south in Germany, in Hesse, a watchman would be stationed on a high tower to signal the arrival of the first swallow, whereupon the news would be announced to the public by the magistrates. And in Cornwall, it was the custom to jump in the air on seeing the first bird.

Not only was the return of the swallow welcomed, it was also thought to be auspicious. In Scotland it was lucky to see the first swallow, although only if you were sitting down at the time. As the early-nineteenth-century writer John MacTaggart explained:

> . . . when we are sitting, the first time we see the swallow flying; walking, when we first hear the cuckoo; and the first foal we meet with, if it be before the eyes of its mother, that will be a fortunate year.

In Bohemia, if a young woman saw a single swallow in the spring for the first time it was thought that she would be married during the year. However, if she saw two then she would remain a spinster.

The precise time that the first swallow arrived was a matter of considerable speculation. People in Brittany, for example, firmly believed that swallows would be sure to arrive before Maundy Thursday so as to be present at the commemoration of the Crucifixion on Good Friday. This belief was probably connected to the tradition held in several countries that the swallow had tried to remove the crown of thorns from Christ's head. In doing so, the bird pricked himself, and the result was the red patch of feathers on the bird's throat and forehead (*compare* ROBIN). An alternative explanation for the red feathers originated in Portugal, where it was believed that the bird tried to wipe away the blood from Jesus' wounds. Yet another version has been recorded in Russia, where it was believed that the swallows also attempted to remove the nails from the Cross.

All the traditions mentioned so far are European ones, but the swallow has had a role to play in many other cultures as well. The ancient Chinese, for example, believed (just as the Romans did) that it was especially lucky if swallows nested on a house, and unlucky if they flew away. People even went to the length of erecting special nesting ledges to encourage the birds to stay. When rain was needed, the Chinese would throw swallows into water to attract the attention of the water spirits. They also believed that the swallow had been sent from heaven to help found the Shang dynasty (*c.*1600–1027 BC), bringing the egg that the dynasty's ancestral mother swallowed in order to conceive. On a more practical note, people who had recently eaten roasted swallow were advised not to cross water in case dragons, which were believed to be very partial to the dish, rose from the depths and attacked them. Traditions about swallows are found in Africa, too. In Southern Africa, the Nguni peoples (including the Zulu, Swazi, Mpondo and Bomvana tribes) describe swallows as 'Intaka Zanzi' ('birds of the home') sent by the tribe's ancestors to comfort the living with promises of future riches.

Even in the remotest regions of the Arctic, myths and legends concerning the swallow abound. The Inuit believed that swallows were the spirits of children taken while making 'play house' igloos near the cliffs, and thought that when the swallows returned to make their nests on the rocks, they were recalling the childish joy of their previous existence. Even today, children like to watch the swallows building their *iglviaks* (miniature igloos). In Russia, it was also thought that the souls of dead children returned to earth in the guise of swallows, and that the birds' twittering song was their chatter.

In the Muslim world, the swallow was held to be a very praiseworthy bird. The story is told in the Koran of swallows attacking a Christian Abyssinian army that was besieging Mecca:

Did He [Allah] not confound their strategem and send against them flocks of birds [swallows] which pelted them with clay-stones, so that they became like the withered stalks of plants which cattle have devoured?

Some scholars have pointed out the word for 'clay-stones' can also be translated as 'smallpox scabs', so it could be that the swallows were credited with striking the enemy army down with disease.

Not all stories about swallows are positive, however. The Greek historian Plutarch, for example, records an incident involving the birds that presaged Cleopatra's defeat at the battle of Actium in 31 BC:

And in Cleopatra's admiral-galley, which was called the *Antonias*, a most inauspicious omen occurred. Some swallows had built in the stern of the galley, but other swallows came, beat the first away, and destroyed their nests.

In the mountains of the Caucasus, the inhabitants believed that all migratory birds brought sickness with them when they returned in the springtime. To avoid this danger, people were advised to drink a glass of wine or a sip of brandy when swallows were seen – an appealing antidote that no doubt helped the belief to persist. In France, there was even a belief that if a swallow flew under a cow's belly, the cow's milk would turn to blood. This belief has a strange sort of parallel in the folklore of the north of England, where it was recorded that if eggs were stolen from a swallow's nest, then any cows in the byre would give bloody milk (the way to cure the cow of this condition was to sprinkle the milk at a crossroads). Also from the north of England comes the belief that if a swallow flew down the chimney this foretold the death of a member of that household and that if it alighted on somebody then their death would follow. If a great many swallows gathered together on the roof of a house in Norfolk this foretold death, since the departing spirit was thought to fly away with the birds. If they gathered on a church roof, it was said that they were discussing who would die before they returned in the spring.

A more positive story about the swallow's supposed gift of prophecy is recorded by Arrian of Nicomedia. During the siege of Halicarnassus by Alexander the Great (356–323 BC), Arrian records, a swallow entered Alexander's tent and:

. . . flew about over his [Alexander's] head loudly twittering, and perched now on this side of his couch and now on that, chirping more noisily than usual. On account of his fatigue he could not be roused from sleep, but being disquieted by the sound he brushed her away gently with his hand. But though struck she was so far from trying to escape that she perched upon the very head of the king, and did not desist until he was wide awake.

Thinking this event could be of significance, Alexander summoned his augur, Aristander the Telmissian, who revealed that it meant that a friend would be disloyal but that the treachery would be discovered in time.

As with a number of other birds that have red in their plumage, swallows were believed to have brought the gift of fire to earth from the gods, an idea that, in the case of the swallow, seems to have originated in Asia and Eastern Europe. Some of the stories told also ingeniously sought to account for the swallow's forked tail at the same time. The Buriat peoples of Siberia, for example, related that when the swallow stole fire from heaven, Tengri, the sky god, fired an arrow at it, hitting the bird and removing its central tail feathers. Consequently, it ended up not only with red on its plumage but with an unusual-shaped tail. In the Baltic countries, it was said that the devil threw a firebrand after the swallow as it flew away and that the red marks on the bird's head and its forked tail show where it was burnt. And in yet another version, it was argued that Satan entrusted the sparrow with the task of guarding fire and that when the swallow swooped down and stole it, the sparrow plucked a few feathers from its tail as it escaped. Two other legends that should be recorded here both come from the Middle East, the first dealing with the forked tail, the second with the red plumage. The first tells how the wicked serpent Eblish snapped at the swallow's tail. The second, from Jewish folklore, claims that when a great fire broke out in the temple in Jerusalem, swallows helped to extinguish it by bringing water in their bills, but were singed in the process.

Throughout Britain and much of Europe, there has long been a great swirl of myth and superstition about the magical 'swallow stone'. Swallow stones, it would seem, were rather like the magic stones which were said to be found in RAVEN's nests, and it is highly probable that all these myths sprang from a common source. There are several variations on the story.

One version is that swallows knew where to find the one magic pebble on a beach that could cure blindness. If you wanted to obtain the pebble for yourself, you had first to blind the nestlings of a pair of swallows, so that the females would fly off to get the magic stone and touch their nestlings' eyes with it in order to restore their sight. Then you had to place a red cloth beneath the nest, so that the swallow would drop the stone on to it, believing that she was dropping it into a fire. Longfellow refers to this belief in his poem *Evangeline* (1847):

Oft in the barns they climbed to the populous nests in the rafters,
Seeking with eager eyes that wondrous stone, which the swallow
Brings from the shore of the sea to restore the sight of the
    fledglings;
Lucky was he who found the stone in the nest of the swallow!

In another version, recorded by Pliny the Elder in the first century AD, the swallow stone, or *chelidonias*, could be found in the stomach of the eldest of a brood, provided it was sought before, or at the time of, the August full moon. And in yet another version, from the Austrian Tyrol, it could be found only in a nest that had been occupied for seven consecutive years. Ironically, given the obsession with this bird and magic stones, it happens to be that swallows are among the few birds of their size who do not ingest small stones and grit to help them grind up hard lumps of food.

It was not only the swallow's stone that was thought to have medicinal qualities. Swallows' ashes mixed with honey were supposed to cure dim sight and bleary vision. Eating a swallow's heart was said to cure drunkenness and the bite of a mad dog in ancient Assyria; to be a remedy for kidney ailments in China (as far back as the fifth century); and to cure epilepsy in Greece. The Greeks also thought that swallows' hearts would cure stuttering and other speech impediments – on the basis that these conditions bore a resemblance to the swallow's twittering song.

Finally, Pliny the Elder records a useful though rather elaborate cure for a headache. The head of a swallow seen feeding in the morning should, he says, be cut off at the full moon, tied in a linen bag and hung up to dry. Then it should be ground up and taken as a medicine. One can't help feeling that by the time the sufferer had prepared this unpleasant concoction the headache would have disappeared of its own volition.

Swan
(Cygnus Olor)

A very large and heavy waterbird that is almost entirely white. The swan flies with its neck outstretched and with regular slow beats of its wings.

Few birds have inspired as many stories as the swan, and it is often very difficult to disentangle what might be termed 'genuine' legends – in other words, traditional stories that have been passed on via oral tradition – from the later literary inventions of authors and composers. In many cases, of course, writers reworked and elaborated elements of existing folk tales. Tchaikovsky's ballet *Swan Lake* (1877), for example, derives ultimately from a German legend about a beautiful girl turned into a swan by a wicked magician. Wagner's opera *Lohengrin* (1848), in which Duke Gottfried suffers a similar fate, owes much to medieval German romance.

That said, there are clearly some swan legends that are very ancient indeed. Probably the oldest of all comes from India and concerns Urvasi, a nymph who was expelled from heaven by Lord Brahma. The legend tells how, on earth, she fell in love with a mortal man, Puruvaras, and agreed to stay with him on the condition that she never saw him naked. A jealous god tricked Puruvaras into breaking this taboo and Urvasi had no choice but to flee from him. However, Puruvaras was determined to track her down and, after much searching, he eventually found her swimming with other nymphs, all in the form

of swans. In some versions of the myth Puruvaras was granted immortality to remain with Urvasi, while in others she refused to return to him. Similar stories can be found in Babylonian and Egyptian mythology, in the myths of Greece and Rome (which also famously offer the story of Leda, wife of the King of Sparta, who was seduced by Zeus in the form of a swan), and as far afield as the Inuit people of Greenland and the Samoyedes of eastern Siberia.

Ireland offers a particularly rich tradition of swan-maiden stories. Indeed, Ireland was even described by a seventeenth-century poet as 'the swan abounding land'. The myths follow a fairly regular pattern: a group of swans fly in and land on a lake, where they remove their feathers and become beautiful maidens, who proceed to bathe in the water. They are usually secretly observed by a young man, who steals the feathered garments of one of the swans and eventually succeeds in making her his wife. Some time later she retrieves her feather clothes and flies away as a white swan.

In a Siberian version of this basic tale, three swans fly on to a lake and assume the form of young women. They leave their feather garments on the shore, where they are found and stolen by a hunter who later marries one of the girls. One day she finds her feather costume, puts it on and flies away through the smoke hole in their tent. As she leaves, she asks her husband to honour her memory with a special ceremony when the swans fly north in spring and in the autumn when they return. The Buriat people who told this story believed that an EAGLE was the father of their people and that the mother goddess was a swan.

One of the best-known of the Irish swan myths tells the tale of the four children of Lir – Finnguala, Āed, Fiachra and Conn – who were cursed by their jealous stepmother, Aífe, and turned into swans. They retained the ability to speak, however, and consoled themselves with poetry and songs, which people from all over Ireland flocked to hear. After nine hundred years the spell was broken, but the children were too old to return to human form and so became pillars of dust. Another myth from Ireland is called *Tochmarc Étaíne*, 'The Wooing of Étaíne', and it seems to have its origins in the eighth century. Étaíne was originally married to Midir, lord of the *sídh* (underworld), but was turned into a butterfly by his first wife, Fuamnach, before being reborn as a princess and then marrying Eochaid, a legendary High King of Ireland who ruled in the second century BC. One day, Midir decided that he wanted Étaíne back, so he entered the castle at Tara to claim her. King Eochaid, unsurprisingly, refused to let her go. A few weeks later, Midir returned in disguise, and challenged Eochaid to the chess-like game of fidchell. By deliberately losing the first three games, Midir was able to trick Eochaid into agreeing that the prize for winning the fourth game should be a kiss from Étaíne. Midir, of course, won easily, and the dismayed Eochaid told him to return in a month to collect his prize. When the appointed time came, Midir found that the castle was surrounded by armed men, but because the terms of the bet were binding, Eochaid was eventually forced to let him through. Midir bent down to kiss Étaíne and then swept her up in his arms, flying away through the smoke hole in the roof of the castle. When onlookers described the scene they said they could see two swans, linked together by chains of gold about their necks, disappearing into the distance.

The myth that some swans were in reality bewitched maidens accords well with the belief that the souls of the dead lived on in swans, particularly the souls of women who had died as virgins. So, not unnaturally, ill fortune was thought to attend anyone who killed a swan. At Corafin in County Clare, the

Birds of a feather

Feathers feature widely in popular superstition, but their significance varies enormously according to the species of bird involved. Since late Victorian times many people have believed that peacock feathers are unlucky if worn or brought indoors, but treating kingfisher feathers in a similar way is thought to heighten the wearer's beauty. Wren feathers are regarded as very lucky: sailors formerly used to carry a feather from a wren slain on New Year's Day to guard against shipwrecks.

Some superstitions apply very specifically to the type of feathers used to stuff pillows and mattresses. At one time, sewing a swan's feather into a husband's pillow was thought to be the best way to ensure that he remained faithful. Pigeon or game bird feathers in the pillow or mattress of an invalid, by contrast, were regarded with great trepidation and, if discovered, were removed for fear that they would lead to a long-drawn-out and painful death.

inhabitants believed that if a swan was killed on Lough Inchiquin then one of the villagers would die, while several thousand miles away in Siberia, even pointing at a swan was judged to be irreverent. Anyone who dared to kill one could be put to death.

The birds were also highly regarded in the Hebrides, especially on the isle of Benbecula. Here it was thought that if you heard the swans calling on a Friday, this foretold good fortune – unless they called at dusk, in which case bad luck would follow. It was also thought that the height at which the birds flew was prophetic: the higher they flew, the greater the good fortune that would come to the islanders.

One of the strangest and most widespread beliefs about the swan was that the bird could foretell the time of its death and would sing sweetly beforehand. Several Greek writers describe this, including Aristotle, who records:

> They are musical and sing chiefly at the approach of death. At this time they fly out to the sea, and men when sailing past the coast of Libya have fallen in with many of them out at sea singing in mournful strains, and have actually seen some of them dying.

The motif of the swan singing before death became a very popular one in later literature. In the final scene of Shakespeare's *Othello*, for example, when Emilia is stabbed by Iago, she tells how 'I will play the swan,/And die in music', while Shakespeare's near contemporary Orlando Gibbons enshrined the idea in one of his madrigals:

The silver swan, who living had no note,
When death approach'd, unlock'd her silent throat;
Leaning her breast against the reedy shore,
Thus sung her first and last, and sung no more.
Farewell, all joys; O Death, come close mine eyes;
More geese than swans now live, more fools than wise.

The belief was still popular over two hundred years later when Byron wrote his poem 'The Isles of Greece', which contains the lines:

Place me on Sunium's marbled steep,
Where nothing, save the waves and I,
May hear our mutual murmurs sweep;
There, swanlike, let me sing and die:

It's intriguing to know how this myth arose. One possibility is that people were entranced by the rather beautiful calls of the whooper and Bewick's swans (as opposed to the more familiar mute swan, which produces only grunts and hisses). When these calls are heard drifting down from a flock of swans flying overhead, the effect can be very evocative. It is also worth considering the following eyewitness account of the death of a swan, given in 1898 by the eminent American zoologist Daniel Giraud Elliot after a shooting trip:

On receiving his wound the wings became fixed and he began at once his song which continued until the water was reached nearly a mile away. I am perfectly familiar with every note a swan is accustomed to utter but never before or since have I heard anything like those sung by this stricken bird. Most plaintive in character and musical in tone, it sounded at times like the soft running of notes in an octave. And as the sound was borne to us, mellowed by the distance, we stood astonished and could only exclaim, 'We have heard the song of a dying swan'.

Whatever the ultimate truth of the matter, it could well be that it was from such accounts that the word 'swansong' was derived, referring to someone's final grandiose act before death.

Woodpecker
(Picus viridis)

The large green woodpecker is mostly green with a bright red crown; the greater spotted woodpecker is smaller and has a mainly pied plumage with bright crimson under its tail. Both birds have very undulating flight with their wings closed for a time every few beats. The black woodpecker is all black apart from its red crest and, unlike other woodpeckers, flies straight.

In Norse mythology, the woodpecker was the bird of Thor, god of thunder and lightning. Just as Thor had red hair, so the woodpecker has a splash of red on its head. Thor had a magic hammer, Mjolnir; the woodpecker hammers on trees. Thor sent lightning to the earth, often striking trees; woodpeckers' holes resemble the holes made by lightning bolts. The woodpecker

was also associated with the great Scandinavian hero Beowulf, though here the connection is a rather vaguer one, perhaps arising from the similarity between an old German name for the woodpecker, *Bienenwulf*, meaning 'bee-eater', and the name of the hero who slew the monster Grendel and ultimately perished in his battle with a ferocious dragon. Whatever the reason for the link made between the two, it was believed that the bird was a reincarnation of Beowulf.

Various legends sought to account for the woodpecker's

appearance and feeding habits. One story about the black woodpecker (which mainly inhabits Northern Europe) tells how Jesus
and St Peter were walking in the country when they came to
a village where an old lady was baking bread. Her name was
Gertrude and on her head she wore a red cloth cap. As the two
men were hungry, they asked Gertrude if they might have a
small piece of her bread. She agreed and placed a tiny piece of
dough in the oven. To her amazement, the dough expanded so
much that it filled the whole oven, just as in the very similar
story of the old woman and the LAPWING. Far from sharing it
with her guests, however, Gertrude claimed that it was too large
for them and proceeded to place an even smaller piece in the
oven. This, too, grew miraculously, but again Gertrude would
not give it to them. Angered by her lack of generosity, Jesus
turned her into a woodpecker, saying that her only subsistence
would be found between the trunk and bark of the trees and
that she would drink only when it rained. Gertrude immediately flew away up the chimney, turning as black as soot as she
did so, though the red cloth cap remained unstained and can
still be seen as the red crest on the black woodpecker's head.
In Sweden, the black woodpecker was often referred to as
'Gertrude's fowl'.

A story from Romania seeks to explain the woodpecker's
constant search for insects in the crevices of tree bark. As with
the tale of Gertrude, the protagonists are Jesus and St Peter.
During a journey in the countryside, they began to find the
insects around them particularly annoying. St Peter persuaded
Jesus to collect the insects and put them in a bag, and when
they happened to chance on an old woman in a black cloak and

a red cap, they asked her to throw the bag into the sea. However, curiosity overcame her and she opened the bag, releasing all the insects back into the wild. Jesus, greatly incensed, turned her into a black woodpecker, doomed eternally to search the trees for insects and place them in the bag again.

The green woodpecker is widely known as a rainbird, and various legends seek to supply the reason for this. One Estonian legend relates that when God created the world he decreed that all the birds should dig with their bills so that in time the holes that they made would fill with water and become rivers and lakes. Every bird obeyed with the exception of the woodpecker, who refused to do any work at all and just flew around while the other birds laboured away. When the work was completed, God called the woodpecker to him and said that as it had refused to peck the earth, it would henceforth only peck wood. And since it had not helped to dig the places where the water was stored, it would only be allowed to drink rainwater.

In France, it was believed that the woodpecker is for ever looking upwards at the clouds and crying, 'Pluie, pluie' ('Rain, rain'), so that its bill can catch any drops of rain that fall. In some areas, it is known as *le procurer du meunier*, 'the miller's advocate', because it pleads for rain during a drought as ardently as the owner of a watermill. In point of fact, woodpeckers, like most non-seed-eating birds, obtain most of their liquid requirements from their food. They drink relatively little water.

As for the red flash on a woodpecker's head, this is accounted for in the following way in a story from Poland. At one time, God and the devil were on friendly terms and ploughed their fields together. The devil used horses but God used a wood-pecker. Needless to say, the devil ploughed a great deal more than the Almighty, and so one night God borrowed the devil's horses and finished his field. On seeing this the next day, the devil was very much surprised and, thinking that the wood-pecker was rather better at ploughing than he had previously assumed, asked God if they could swap animals. To the devil's chagrin, he soon found out that he could not make the wood-pecker plough at all, and he became so angry that he struck it, breaking open its head. The red 'wound' has remained on the bird's crown ever since.

Many birds were said to know of certain magical substances that had the power to cure ill and prolong life. In the case of the woodpecker, it was supposed to know of a magic herb, otherwise undiscovered by mankind, called springwort. In Germany, people formerly believed that if the entrance to a woodpecker's nest was blocked up, the bird would straightaway fly off to find the herb and hold it against the obstruction, whereupon a hole would immediately appear. Springwort was therefore ideally suited to open locks. In France, by contrast, it was believed that if people rubbed it on their limbs it would give them superhuman strength.

Not surprisingly, springwort was highly coveted, and various ruses were devised in order to obtain it. One method was to place a piece of red cloth on the ground near a woodpecker's nest. The woodpecker, it was argued, would mistake the cloth for a fire and, thinking that its secret would be consumed in the flames, drop the precious springwort on to the cloth (*compare* SWALLOW). Some believed that springwort actually grew in the nesting hole of the woodpecker. Others held that it had to fly off to find it. Either way, humans could not lay their hands on it without the woodpecker's help.

Wren
(Troglodytes troglodytes)

Tiny, plump bird, mainly russet-brown with a pale breast. It is constantly on the move and has a very loud trilling song that is heard throughout the year.

Despite being one of the smallest and most inconspicuous of European birds, the wren has inspired an impressively large body of beliefs, superstitions and stories. Dominant among these is the belief that to sacrifice the bird on New Year's Day or at the winter solstice would remove or appease the evil forces that lurked at the darkest and coldest time of the year. True, it wasn't only the wren that could be sacrificed to avoid bad luck and ensure good fortune – in Scotland, for example, almost any animal would do, and some Scottish housewives used to slaughter a chicken on New Year's Day; nevertheless, the 'wren hunt' was felt to have a particular potency and achieved widespread popularity.

In France, Wales, Scotland, the Isle of Man and much of Ireland (except Ulster), the wren hunt was usually followed by a procession of some sort. The details varied considerably from place to place, but the essential element of displaying the victim and then sacrificing it in public remained broadly the same everywhere. In the west of Ireland, for example, between four and twenty unmarried men, known as 'wren boys', would first parade the captured bird around the village, possibly having decorated it with ribbons or carrying it on a bush, on a pole in the shape of a cross, on crossed sticks or in a container of some kind — perhaps a small box with a glass cover, a hollowed-out turnip, or an elaborate ribbon-bedecked 'wren-house' with windows and a door. The parade of the wren would then proceed from house to house, usually accompanied by a song or a poem, sometimes in Irish, more often in English. Occasionally the wren boys would dance at some of the homes they visited, and might well be given small amounts of cash or refreshments, which would be divided up among the participants at the end of the ceremony.

At Dingle in County Kerry, Ireland, a very elaborate wren procession still takes place, with upwards of thirty men taking part. Some of these are disguised as women and are called *Oinsigh* (women fools). Others wear straw suits and carry wooden swords or bladders on sticks. The 'wren man' wears a special costume and carries the dead wren (an artificial bird is now used) in a holly bush fixed to a pole, and the 'captain' of the party wears a special green uniform. During the ceremony, a mock battle takes place between the men with wooden swords and the men with bladders on sticks. Further west in County Kerry, the focal point of the annual parade is a make-believe horse with two wren boys hidden inside. This hobby horse is referred to as the *Lair Bhan* or 'White Mare' and has a wooden head with a movable jaw and a white sheet which hangs down to hide the two men inside. Similar rituals involving the wren are recorded in the Balkans and were designed to please the earth gods, so as to ensure a bountiful harvest. Such practices certainly survived within living memory and, like the wren procession at Dingle, may still take place in isolated areas.

The tradition of the wren hunt was also once strong in France, where towards the end of the year in Carcassonne, the 'wren boys' would assemble and go out into the countryside to search for wrens. The first boy to kill a wren was declared to be the king, and the body of the wren was carried back to town on a pole. On 30 December, the king would parade through the streets with all those who had taken part in the wren hunt. All would carrry torches and they would be accompanied by a drum-and-fife band – writing 'Vive le Roi' in chalk on the doors of the houses. On Twelfth Night, the king would dress in a blue mantle, a crown and a sceptre and go to Mass in the parish church of St Vincent. He would be preceded by a man bearing a pole decorated with olive leaves, oak leaves or mistletoe, at the top of which the wren would be affixed. After Mass, the procession would visit the bishop, the mayor, magistrates and other important inhabitants to collect money for a banquet that would be held the same evening and that would be followed by a dance. This ceremony was abolished after the French Revolution, to be revived at the restoration of the Bourbon monarchy and finally suppressed some time after 1830.

In some places, such as Marseilles and Mardillon near Châtillon-sur-Indre, the wren was treated as if it were a creature of huge size. It was brought to the local seigneur with a great rope attached and on a wagon drawn by four black oxen. A similar tradition could be found in parts of England. In Devon, for instance, the wren was borne on a pole carried by two strong men who pretended that they were lifting a great weight. In Gloucestershire, an old song stipulates that three men are required to carry the bird, six to cook it and the entire town to eat it. Other light-hearted ceremonies included one at Villiers in Cher, where newly wedded couples had to visit the steward of the estate on the first Trinity Sunday after their wedding, bearing a wooden receptacle containing a wren; and another in the Upper Limousin, where the wren was carried in a wagon in which couples who had been married for less than seven years sat on one side and couples who had been married longer on the other. Later the two sides would take part in a tug of war.

Alongside all these traditions was a belief that wrens' feathers acted as a talisman against various perils, especially those at sea. But it has to be said that the wren had a sinister aspect, too. Manx fishermen thought that a sea sprite haunted shoals of herring and conjured up storms before flying away in the form of a wren. The nineteenth-century writer and antiquarian Joseph Train elaborated on this myth in his *History of the Isle of Man*:

In former times a fairy of uncommon beauty exerted such undue influence over the male population that she at various times induced by her sweet voice numbers to follow her footsteps till by degrees she led them to the sea where they perished. This barbarous exercise of power had continued for a great length of time till it was apprehended that the island would be exhausted of its defenders; when a knight errant sprang up, who discovered some means of countervailing the charms used by this siren, and even laid a plot for her destruction which she only escaped at the moment of extreme hazard by taking the form of a wren. But though she evaded instant annihilation, a spell was cast upon her by which she was condemned, on every succeeding New-year's-day, to reanimate the same form with the definitive sentence that she must ultimately perish by human hand. In consequence of this *well authenticated* legend, on the specified anniversary, every man and boy in the Island (except those who have thrown off the trammels of superstition), devote the hours between sun-rise and sun-set, to the hope of extirpating the fairy.

This reputation for untrustworthiness can be found elsewhere. One Christian myth, for example, blamed the wren for exposing Jesus in the Garden of Gethsemane by revealing his whereabouts with its loud ticking call. In Ireland, the bird was believed to have betrayed Irish troops by hopping around on a soldier's drum during a planned stealth attack on Cromwell's army. In Denmark, a myth exists about a Danish raiding party that was similarly betrayed. A further myth tells how the wren awoke the men guarding the first Christian martyr, St Stephen, just at the moment he was about to escape.

That said, in general the wren, like the SWALLOW and the ROBIN, was considered a bird that should be protected rather than shunned, and it was held that its nest should be left well alone. One traditional saying warned that:

> He that hurts a robin or a wren
> Will never prosper on sea or land.

Or, in the words of a better-known rhyme:

> The robin red-breast and the wren
> Are God Almighty's cock and hen.

Wryneck
(Jynx torquilla)

A small migrant bird closely related to the woodpecker. Its colouring is mottled brown with a dark band running down from the back of its head to its back. It has two toes pointing forward and two backwards.

The wryneck was a familiar sight in Europe in the nineteenth century, but numbers fell steadily throughout the twentieth century and today they are very difficult birds to spot. Its most striking characteristic, from which it derives its name, is its ability to twist and writhe its neck up to 180 degrees in a distinctly snake-like manner, frequently accompanying this action with a loud hissing sound in order to warn off predators. The bird came to be closely associated not only with snakes but also – not surprisingly, given the somewhat threatening nature of its behaviour – with witchcraft as well. In fact, the Latin name for the wryneck, *Jynx*, gives us the word 'jinx' – a person or thing cursed in some way to bring bad luck.

The wryneck's sinister reputation may well have been re-inforced by the strongly held belief that it displayed quite extraordinary cunning when catching its prey. It was thought to lie down near an ants' nest with its eyes shut and its tongue protruding, pretending to be dead. The ants would then confidently assume that they could wander all over it and some would enter its bill, only to find that it snapped shut around

them. Sadly, the reality is less exciting. Any close observation will reveal that a wryneck snaps up ants with its bill or extracts them from their nest using its sticky tongue. It doesn't have to resort to any sort of subterfuge.

Because people believed that the bird could charm ants into its mouth, they thought it might also be able to charm back errant lovers. The outcome of this optimistic view was the extremely cruel practice of trapping the bird, and then nailing it, spread-eagled, to four spokes of a wheel. The wheel would then be spun round while special incantations were intoned. The ancient Greek poet Theocritus mentions this procedure in his *Second Idyll*, telling how a lovelorn woman, in an attempt to entice back her faithless lover, called out, 'Wryneck, bring back that man of mine to my house.' Some wryneck wheels in ancient Greece were finely made, and one, supposedly invented by Aphrodite, the goddess of love, was said to be chased with gold. It was a wryneck wheel that was used to make Medea fall in love with Jason, as the great lyric poet Pindar recorded:

But she of Cyprus, queen of swiftest darts, yoking the dappled wryneck all asprawl to the inescapable wheel, brought down from Olympus the bird of madness for the first time among men and taught Aeson's wise son [Jason] the prayer charms.

The spell worked completely on Medea: she fell in love with Jason and had two children with him. But when he left her to marry the daughter of the King of Creon she was gripped with a murderous and frightful rage, and exacted her revenge by killing his bride and murdering the children.

The wryneck also features in another Greek myth which tells how the nymph Iynx took her revenge on the goddess Hera – who had stolen her voice and given it to Echo – by making Hera's husband Zeus fall in love with Io, who was one of Hera's priestesses. However, when Hera discovered what Iynx had done, she turned her into a wryneck; hence, ultimately, the bird's Latin name.

The bird's arrival in the spring was often linked with that of the CUCKOO, and in England the wryneck has also been known as the cuckoo's mate, the cuckoo's messenger or the cuckoo's leader. Because it was thought to arrive while the barley was being sown, it was known as the barley snake bird in Hampshire. In the same county, it was said that the wryneck ordered his coat at Beaulieu Fair (15 April) and put it on at Downton Fair (23 April). This is a piece of pure whimsy: the bird's plumage undergoes no changes at all during the spring.

Authors quoted or mentioned in the text

Abu ar-Rayhan Muhammad ibn Ahmad al-Biruni	(973–1048) Islamic scholar
Aelian	(*c.* AD 175–235) Roman biographer and naturalist
Aesop	(*c.*550 BC) Greek writer of fables
Albertus Magnus	(13th century) German cleric
Aldrovandi, Ulisse	(1522–1605) Italian naturalist
Apollonius	(*c.*295–215 BC) Greek poet
Aristophanes	(*c.*448–*c.*385 BC) Greek comic dramatist
Aristotle	(384–322 BC) Greek poet, philosopher and teacher
Armstrong, Edward A.	(1900–1978) cleric and academic ornithologist
Avraham ben David ha-Levi, Rabbi	(*c.*1110–*c.*1180) Spanish historian and philosopher
Boorde, Andrew	(1490–1549) doctor and traveller
Browne, Sir Thomas	(1605–82) English writer and physician
Budge, Sir E. A. W.	(1857–1934) Egyptologist and expert on Assyria
Buffon, Count Georges	(1707–88) French naturalist
Carmichael, Alexander	(1832–1912) Scottish folklorist
Cervantes, Miguel de	(1547–1616) Spanish writer

Chaucer, Geoffrey	(c.1345–1400) English author
Chester, Robert	(1566–1640) English poet
Cicero	(106–43 BC) Roman orator and statesman
Columella	(c. AD 65) Roman writer on agricultural matters
Dionysius of Halicarnassus	(c.60–7 BC) Greek writer living in Rome
Drayton, Michael	(1563–1631) English poet
Dryden, John	(1631–1700) English poet
Elliot, Daniel Giraud	(1835–1915) American ornithologist
Elmocadessi, Azz'Eddin	Persian poet
Farid ud-Din Attar	(c.1142–c.1220) Persian poet
Gerard, John	(1545–1612) English herbalist
Giraldus Cambrensis	(c.1146–1220) cleric and traveller
Gesner, Conrad	(1516–65) Swiss naturalist
Gibbons, Orlando	(1583–1625) English composer
Hadasi, Judah	(12th century) Jewish writer
Horapollo	(4th century AD) Greek writer
Hoskyns-Abrahall, John	(19th century) English writer
Ibrahim ibn Ahmed al-Turtushi	(10th century) Moorish diplomat
Isidore of Sevill	(7th century) Spanish cleric and naturalist
Jerome, St	(c.342–420) Christian ascetic and scholar
Johnson, Richard	(1573–?1659) English romance writer
Johnson, Samuel	(1709–84) English writer and lexicographer

Jonson, Ben	(1572–1637) poet and dramatist
Lobel, Matthias de	(1538–1616) Flemish naturalist
Longfellow, Henry W.	(1807–82) American poet
Lyly, John	(c.1554–1606) English dramatist and novelist
MacTaggart, John	(1791–1830) Scottish writer
Marlowe, Christopher	(1564–93) English dramatist
Milton, John	(1608–74) English poet
Musa ud Damiri	(14th century) Egyptian scholar
Odoric, Friar	(14th century) monk and traveller
Ovid	(43 BC–AD 17) Roman poet
Pindar	(c.518–c.438 BC) Greek lyric poet
Pliny the Elder	(AD 23–79) Roman writer and naturalist
Plutarch	(c. AD 46–120) Greek historian, biographer and philosopher
Rolland, Eugene	(1806–1909) French author
Shakespeare, William	(1564–1616) English poet and dramatist
Sidney, Sir Philip	(1554–86) soldier and poet
Swan, John	(d. 1671) English doctor and clergyman
Theocritus	(3rd century BC) Greek poet
Titinius	(c.190–c.160 BC) Greek comic dramatist
Topsell, Edward	(1572–1625) English naturalist
Train, Joseph	(1779–1852) English antiquarian
Tulloch, Bobby	(1929–96) Scottish naturalist
Turner, Sir William	(16th century) ornithologist

Vincent de Beauvais	(c.1190–1264) French Dominican scholar
Webster, John	(c.1580– c.1625) English dramatist
White, Gilbert	(1720–93) cleric and naturalist
Whittier, John Greenleaf	(1807–92) American Quaker poet
Willughby, Francis	(1635–72) English naturalist
Yeats, William Butler	(1865–1939) Irish poet

Gods and goddesses

GREEK	ROMAN	NORDIC
Athene *Goddess of Wisdom*	Minerva	
Aphrodite *Goddess of Love*	Venus	
Ares *God of War*	Mars	Odin/Wotan. Later replaced by Thor/Donar, God of Thunder
Demeter *Corn Goddess*	Ceres	
Hephaestus *God of Fire*	Vulcan	
Hera *Queen of Goddesses*	Juno	Frigg/Frija
Hermes *God of Travellers*	Mercury	
Zeus *King of the Gods*	Jupiter/Jove	

Bibliography

Almquist, B., pers. comm., 1990

Armstrong, E. A., *The Folklore of Birds* (London, 1958)

Armstrong, E. A., *The Life and Lore of the Bird* (New York, 1975)

Ayto, J., *Brewer's Dictionary of Phrase and Fable*, seventeenth edn (HarperCollins, 2005)

Brown, W. J., *The Gods Had Wings* (London, 1936)

Bynon, J., 'North African Bird Lore: New Light on Old Problems' *Folklore*, 98 (1987)

Costello, L. S., *The Rose Garden of Persia* (London, 1899)

Dawood, N. J. (trans.), *The Koran* (London, 2003)

Greenoak, F., *All the Birds of the Air* (London, 1979)

Guirand, F. (ed.), *New Larousse Encyclopaedia of Mythology*, English edn (London, 1959)

Hare, C. E., *Bird Lore* (London, 1952)

Ingersoll, E., *Birds in Fable, Legend and Folklore* (New York, 1923)

Lack, D., *Robin Redbreast* (Oxford, 1950)

Lockwood, W. B., *The Oxford Book of British Bird Names* (Oxford, 1984)

McGee, W. J., 'The Seri Indians', *Report of U.S. Bureau of Ethnology 1885–6* (Washington, 1898)

Meyer, K., *The Voyage of Bran* (London, 1895)

Pollard, J., *Birds in Greek Life and Myth* (London, 1977)

Raven, C. E., *English Naturalists from Neckham to Ray* (Cambridge, 1947)

Rolland, E., *Faune Populaire de la France*, vol. II (Paris, 1879)

Roud, S., *The Penguin Guide to the Superstitions of Britain and Ireland* (London, 2003)

Swann, H. K., *A Dictionary of English and Folk-names of British Birds* (London, 1913)

Swire, O. F., *The Outer Hebrides and their Legends* (Edinburgh, 1966)

Sydow, C. W. von, *Selected Papers on Folklore* (Copenhagen, 1948)

Ticehurst, C. D., *A History of the Birds of Suffolk* (London, 1932)

Topsell, E., *The Fowles of Heaven or History of Birdes* (Austin, 1972)

Tulloch, B., 'The Eagle and the Baby', *Scots Magazine* (1978)

Index

Abyssinia, 4
Achaeans, 67
Actium, battle of, 137–8
adultery, 29
Āed, 145
Aedon, Queen of
  Thebes, 83
Aelian, 18, 163
Aesop, 57, 163
Africa, 14, 48, 58, 94–5,
  136–7
Agathokles, 97
Aïfe, 145
Aigypios, 90, 91
al-Biruni (Abu ar-
  Rayhan Muhammad
  ibn Ahmad al-Biruni),
  57, 163
Alaska, 15, 33–4, 115
Albertus Magnus, 46–7,
  95, 98, 163
Alcedo atthis see king-
  fisher
alcohol, 98–9
Aldrovandi, Ulisse, 55,
  163
Alexander the Great,
  138–9
Algonquin tribe, 33
Allah, 10, 75, 137
Amish, 98
Andalusia, 112
Anderson, William, 49
Annunciation Day, 24

Anser anser see goose
Aphrodite, 6, 36–7, 161,
  167
Apollo, 5, 42, 114
Apollonius, 39, 163
apotheosis ceremony, 43
Aquila chrysaetos see
  eagle
Arawak Indians, 13
Arcadia, 1
Arctic, 53, 137
Ares, 5–6, 167
Argonauts, 39
Argos, 29
Argus, 101
Aristander the
  Telmissian, 139
Aristophanes, 163
  The Wasps, 97
Aristotle, 47, 88, 105,
  108, 147, 163
  *The History of
  Animals*, 1, 15, 69
Arizona, 93
Armstrong, Edward A.,
  50, 114, 163
Arnoldus, 18
Arrian of Nicomedia,
  138–9
Artemis, 114
Arthur, King, 32–3
Arthurian legend, 29
Ashtoroth, 35–6
Asia, 31, 70, 99, 139

Asmodi, 50
Assyria, 141
Astarte, 36, 37
Atagartis, 36
Athene, 97, 167
Atlas mountains, 48
augury and divination,
  6–7, 52, 67 *see also*
  omens/predicting the
  future
Augustus, Emperor, 93
auk, little, 56
Aulis, 67
Austrian Tyrol *see* Tyrol
Austro-Hungarian
  Empire, 45
Avraham ben David ha-
  Levi, Rabbi, 163
  *Sefer ha-Qabbalah
  (Book of Tradition)*,
  46

'Babes in the Wood',
  122
babies and children, 20,
  34, 48–9, 94–5, 97,
  130–1, 132, 137
Babylonians, 45, 144
Balkans, 156
Baltic countries, 139
basilisks, 11
battles/war, 39–40,
  44
Bavaria, 52, 60

Bayley, Harold: *The Lost Language of Symbolism*, 57
Beaulieu Fair, 162
Bedouin, 13
bee-eaters, carmine, 14
Benbecula, 147
Beowulf, 150
Berbers, 94–5
bird droppings, 127
bittern, 58
Black Sea, 39
blackbird, 1–4, 20
blindness, cure for, 34, 140
Bloody Bertha (Berchta), 51
Bohemia, 28, 40, 64–5, 135
Bomvana, 136–7
Boorde, Andrew, 163
   Book of Knowledge, 85
Boulis, 90, 91
Brahma, 57, 142
Brescia, 1
Britain, 7, 24, 26, 51–2, 53, 67, 75, 76–9, 85, 86–7, 98, 113, 130, 140
   see also England; Scotland; Wales; names of counties
Brittany, 59, 67, 87, 120, 122, 123, 126, 135–6
Brompton Bruan Fair, 24
Browne, Sir Thomas, 70–1, 163
   Enquiries into Vulgar and Common Errors, 86
Budge, Sir E.A.W., 163
   Syrian Anatomy, Surgery and Therapeutics, 61–2
Buffon, Count Georges, 108, 163
Buriat people, 32–3, 139, 144
Burma, 10–11
bustard, kori, 14
Byron, Lord: 'The Isles of Greece', 148

Cader Idris, 45
calls and songs
   blackbird, 3
   cockerel, 4, 10, 11
   cuckoo, 25–7
   diver, 34
   hoopoe, 58–9
   lapwing, 73, 75
   nightingale, 81–4, 85, 86, 87
   nightjar, 88, 90
   owl, 94
   peacock, 102
   pelican, 104
   quail, 110
   swan, 148–9
calygreyhound, 48
Cambridgeshire, 28
Canada, 33, 34
Candlemas, 4
Capitol, 93
Caprimulgus europaeus see nightjar
Carcassonne, 156–7

Carmichael, Alexander, 130, 163
Carthaginians, 97
Catholic Church, 54
cattle, 58, 88–90
Caucasus, 138
Caucasus, Mount, 43
Cervantes, Miguel de, 164
   Don Quixote, 32–3
Ceyx, King of Trachis, 71, 72
Chang-hko, 10–11
Channel Islands, 40
Chaucer, Geoffrey, 164
   Parlement of Fowles, 41, 91
Cher, 157
Cherokees, 16–17, 97, 116
Chester, Robert, 164
   Love's Martyr, 102
childbirth, 7, 8, 47, 61–2, 117
children *see* babies and children
China/Chinese
   and crane, 15–16
   and goose, 50, 51
   and hoopoe, 60
   and house sparrow, 64
   and owl, 98
   and peacock, 101–2
   and raven, 113
   and stork, 33, 132
   and swallow, 136, 141
Chipcase, 126
Christian associations
   cockerel, 9–10

crossbill, 21–2
dove, 37–8
eagle, 44
house sparrow, 65–6
lapwing, 73–4
magpie, 79–80, 120
owl, 99
pelican, 104–5
robin, 120–1
stork, 133
swallow, 135–6
woodpecker, 151–2
wren, 159
Christmas, 22
churches, 9, 10, 44
Cicero, 113, 164
 De Natura Deorum
 (*On the Nature of the
 Gods*), 6–7
Ciconia ciconia see stork
Claudius, Publius, 6–7
Cleopatra, 137–8
Clovis, King, 38
cockatrice, 11
cockerel, 4–11
Columella, 164
 De Re Rustica, 98
Commodus Antonius,
 Emperor, 93
Conn, 145
Coptic Church, 4
Corafin, 146–7
corn, 6, 64–5, 122
corncrake, 108, 129
Cornwall, 24, 27, 125–6,
 135
corpses, 122–3
Corvus corax see raven
Corvus frugilegus see rook

Coturnix coturnix see
 quail
counter-spells, 78–9
County Clare, 146–7
County Kerry, 156
County Meath, 3
crane, 11–18
creation stories, 30–1,
 35, 74, 115
Cromwell, Oliver, 43
crossbill, 19–22
crow, 32
Crow Indians, 13
Crucifixion, 21–2, 66,
 74, 80, 120–1, 136
cuckold, 29
cuckoo, 22–9, 60, 86–7,
 129, 162
Cuculus canorus see
 cuckoo
curlew, 66
Cygnus Olor see swan
Cyllene, Mount, 1
Cyranides, 98–9
Czechoslovakia, 109

dead people *see* corpses;
 funerals; graves; souls
 of the dead
death, 11, 26, 66, 67,
 91–2, 93, 112, 113,
 126, 138, 146, 147
Denmark/Danes, 25–6,
 28, 73–4, 75, 159
Derbyshire, 28
devil, 38, 80, 152–3
Devon, 118, 127, 157
Dingle, 156
Dionysius of

Halicarnassus, 105–6,
 108–9, 164
diver, 30–5
divination/augury, 6–7,
 52, 67 *see also*
 omens/predicting the
 future
Dot-son-paa, 115
dove, 35–41, 79
Downton Fair, 162
Drayton, Michael, 164
 The Owl, 123
Dresden, 81
drunkenness, 98, 141
Dryden, John, 43–4, 164

eagle, 8, 41–9, 116
Easter, 22, 126, 127
Ebeling, 13
Eblish, 140
Echo, 162
Edward the Confessor,
 85
eggs, golden, 57
Egypt/Egyptians, 13, 16,
 50, 57, 62, 93, 144
Elliot, Daniel Giraud,
 148–9, 164
Elmocadessi, Azz'Eddin,
 103, 164
England, 28, 53, 78, 124,
 125–6, 138, 157, 162
 see also Britain; names
 of counties
Eochaid, 145
epilepsy, 9, 19, 81, 99,
 108, 119, 141
Erithacus rubecula see
 robin

Essex, 11, 85, 118–19
Estonia, 152
Étaíne, 145–6
Ethon, 43
Eucharist, 104
Europe, 7, 12, 20, 26, 58, 60, 63, 70, 72, 79, 86–7, 88–9, 95, 98, 100, 104, 131, 132, 136, 139, 140, 160 *see also* names of countries
evil eye, 101

Fabian, Pope, 38
Faeroe Islands, 30, 33, 34
Far East, 52
Farid ud-Din Attar, 164
    Mantiq at-Tayr (The Conference of Birds), 62–3
Feast of St Benedict, 24
Feast of St Philip and St James, 25
Feast of St Valerian and St Tiburtius, 25
feathers, 93, 101–2, 146, 158
fertility, 7, 50–1, 131
Fetlar, 48–9
Fiachra, 145
Finland, 109
Finnguala, 145
Finnmark, 35
fire, 20, 43, 98, 116, 118, 124, 139–40
flood stories, 10–11, 37, 68–9, 79–80, 115

food, birds as, 9, 18, 51–2, 107–8
Fourth Lateran Council, 54
France
    and cockerel, 7
    and cuckoo, 24–5, 26, 28
    and eagle, 45
    and magpie, 80–1
    and nightingale, 82
    and owl, 94
    and quail, 110
    and raven, 113
    and robin, 124
    and swallow, 138
    and woodpecker, 152, 153
    and wren, 124, 154, 156–7
    see also names of French regions
Francis of Assisi, St, 82
Frisians, 50
frogs, 128
Fuamnach, 145
funerals, 123
future, prediction of the *see* omens/prediction of the future

Gallus gallus see cockerel
Gauls, 50
Gavia immer see diver
Gerald de Barri *see* Giraldus Cambrensis
Gerard, John, 164
    Herball, 55
Germanicus, 117

Germany
    and blackbird, 4
    and crossbill, 19
    and cuckoo, 25, 26, 28, 60
    and dove, 40
    and goose, 51
    and hoopoe, 58, 60
    and magpie, 81
    and owl, 97
    and raven, 113
    and robin, 123
    and swallow, 135
    and swan, 142
    and woodpecker, 153
Gertrude, 151
Gesner, Conrad, 54, 164
Gethsemane, Garden of, 65, 159
Gibbons, Orlando, 147–8, 164
Giraldus Cambrensis (Gerald of Wales; Gerald de Barri), 70, 164
    Topographia Hiberniae (The Topography of Ireland), 53–4
Gloucestershire, 157
Gmelin, Johann Georg, 13
God, 37, 81–2, 107, 152–3
golden eggs, 57
Good Friday, 136
goose, 50–7
    barnacle, 52–6, 109
    brent, 56
gout, 99
graves, 32, 34, 51

Graves, Mr, 126
Greeks/Greece
  and blackbird, 1
  and cockerel, 5–6
  and crane, 15
  and cuckoo, 29
  and dove, 36–7
  and eagle, 42–3, 48
  and house sparrow, 67
  and kingfisher, 71–2
  and nightingale, 83–4
  and nightjar, 90–1
  and owl, 97, 98
  and peacock, 100–1
  and quail, 108–9
  and raven, 114
  and robin, 121
  and stork, 132
  and swallow, 133–5,
    137–8, 141
  and swan, 144, 147
  and wryneck, 161–2
Greenland, 34, 116, 144
Gregory IX, Pope, 50
Grendel, 150
griffin, 48
Grus grus see crane
Guernsey, 124

Hadasi, Judah, 57, 164
Hagland, Mr, 13–14
Halcyone, 71–2
Halicarnassus, siege of,
  138–9
Hampshire, 89, 162
Harris, 128, 129
harvest, 7, 60, 110
Havering-atte-Bower, 85
headache, cure for, 141

Hebrides, 53, 128,
  129–30, 147
Hecate, 95
hell, 124
hens, 6–7
Hephaestus, 6, 167
Hera, 29, 71, 100, 101,
  162, 167
Heracles, 43
heraldry, 14, 48, 100, 133
Herefordshire, 24
Hermes, 5, 101, 167
Hertfordshire, 120
Hindus, 57
Hirundo rustica see
  swallow
Holland, 96
Holy Ghost, 37
hoopoe, 8, 58–63, 84
hops, 85
Horapollo, 106, 164
Hoskyns-Abrahall, John,
  164
  'The Redbreast, a
    Bretton Legend', 120
house sparrow, 64–7
Hugin, 114
hummingbird, 13, 115
Hungary, 96

Ibrahim ibn Ahmed al-
  Turtushi, 55–6, 164
Inchiquin, Lough, 147
India, 56, 94, 97, 102,
  142
Indian Ocean, 57
Indians, American, 13,
  16–17, 93, 97, 116, 131
Indonesia, 109

Ingersoll, Ernest, 13
Innocent III, Pope, 54
Inuit, 15, 34, 137, 144
invisibility, 8, 110, 117
'invisibility' stone, 8,
  116, 117
Io, 101, 162
Ipiutak, 33–4
Iran, 62–3
Ireland
  and blackbird, 3–4
  and goose, 53
  and raven, 112
  and rook, 128
  and swan, 144,
    145–7
  and wren, 154, 155,
    156, 159
Irish Sea, 56
Islam/Islamic culture,
  10, 38, 62, 137
Isle of Man, 154, 158
Israelites, 107
Italy, 1, 40, 81–2, 109
Itylus, 83
Itys, 84
Iynx, 162

Japan, 39–40
Jason, 39, 161–2
jay, 115
Jerome, St, 104–5, 164
Jerusalem, 40, 140
Jesus
  and cockerel, 9–10
  and crossbill, 21
  and dove, 37
  and house sparrow,
    65, 66

Jesus (*cont.*)
and lapwing, 73–4
and magpie, 120, 121
and owl, 99
and pelican, 104–5
and raven, 116
and robin, 120–1
and stork, 133
and swallow, 66, 136
and woodpecker, 151–2
and wren, 159
Jewish tradition, 55, 57, 94, 140
John the Evangelist, St, 44
Johnson, Richard, 164
Most Famous History of the Seven Champions of Christendom, 122
Johnson, Samuel, 164
Cornucopia, 123
Jonson, Ben, 165
Masque of Queens, 95
Joseph, 37
Juno, 50, 167
Jupiter, 43, 167
Jynx torquilla see wryneck

Kaptor Massar, 38
Kent, 67, 85
Kentigern, St, 121–2
Kevin, St, 3
kingfisher, 67–72, 146
Koran, 137
Koreans, 51
Koronis, 114
Koyukon people, 115

Lair Bahn (White Mare), 156
lammergeyer, 91
Lan Ts'ai-ho, 33
Landebia, 126
Landeyda, 114
Languedoc, 113
lapwing, 72–6, 99, 151
Last Supper, 9–10, 104
Leda, 144
Levantines, 36
Lex Ciconia (stork law), 132
'life' stone, 8, 116, 117
lightning, 4, 20, 98, 118
Limousin, 157
Linwood Grange, 126
Lir, children of, 145
Llandegla, 9
Lobel, Matthias de, 165
Plantarum Seu Stirpium Historia (*History of Plants*), 55
Lohengrin, 142
London, 127
Longfellow, Henry Wadsworth, 165
Evangeline, 140
'The Legend of the Crossbill', 21–2
Looe, 126
Lorraine, 123
Lough Inchiquin, 147
love, 35–7, 70, 87
Loxia curvirostra see crossbill
Luke, Gospel according to, 10

Luscinia luscinia see nightingale
lust, 29
Lyly, John, 165
Euphues, 132

MacTaggart, John, 135, 165
Magic of Kirani, King of Prussia, The, 110
magpie, 1–2, 76–81, 120, 121
Man, Isle of, 154, 158
Mao, Chairman, 64
Mardillon, 157
Marius, Gaius, 44
Mark, King of Cornwall, 29
Marlowe, Christopher, 165
The Jew of Malta, 71, 112
marriage, 25–6, 40, 52, 135
Marseilles, 157
Mary II, Queen, 123
Matthew, Gospel according to, 37
Maundy Thursday, 135
Mecca, 137
Medea, 161–2
medicinal properties
cockerel, 7, 9
crane, 18
crossbill, 19
diver, 34
hoopoe, 61–2
kingfisher, 69–70
magpie, 81

owl, 97–8
quail, 108
swallow, 141
Mesopotamia, 35
Mexico, 103–4
Michaelmas, 51
Middle Ages, 9, 46–7,
  56, 70, 86, 104
Middle East, 38, 56, 58,
  75, 86, 140
Midir, 145–6
migration, 12–13, 108–9,
  129–30
Milton, John, 165
  'To the Nightingale',
  87
Mjolnir, 149
Montana, 13
Morpheus, 71–2
Mosen, Julius, 21
Mount Caucasus, 43
Mount Cyllene, 1
Mount Olympus, 43
Mount Snowdon, 45
Mount Thornax, 29
Mpondo, 136–7
Muhammad, 10
Munin, 114
Musa ud Damiri, 165
  Hayat al-Hayawan
  (*The Life of Animals*),
  16

Napoleonic Empire, 45
Neophron, 90–1
nests
  cuckoo's lack of, 28–9
  kingfisher, 69
  magpie, 80–1

nightingale, 85, 86
stork, 132–3
swallow, 136
New Year's Day, 154
Nguni peoples, 136–7
Nicholson, Robert, 49
Nidderdale, 90
nightingale, 62, 81–7
nightjar, 88–91
Ningirsu, 41
Niobe, 83
Noah, 10, 37, 68, 69
Norfolk, 122, 138
Normandy, 25, 28
Norse mythology, 114,
  118, 149
North Africa, 48, 94–5
North America, 30, 31,
  97 *see also* names of
  places in North
  America
Northumberland, 26–7,
  125–6
Norway, 25, 26, 27, 33,
  34, 35

Odin, 51, 114, 167
Odoric, Friar, 56–7, 165
Old Testament, 37, 63
Olmecs, 17
Olympus, Mount, 43
omens/prediction of the
  future
  cockerel/hen, 6–7
  cuckoo, 25–7
  dove, 40
  eagle, 45
  goose, 52
  house sparrow, 66–7

magpie, 76–9
nightingale, 87
owl, 91–3, 94, 97
raven, 111–13
rook, 125–6
stonechat, 130
stork, 133
swallow, 135, 137–9
swan, 147
  see also death
'Ommer Sunday', 35
opinicus, 48
Orleton Fair, 24
Ovid, 84, 93, 165
owl, 66, 74, 91–9, 108,
  116

Pandion, King of
  Athens, 84
Parnell, Dr Geoff, 113
parrot, 62
Passer domesticus see
  house sparrow
Pavo cristatus see
  peacock
Pawpaw Nan-chaung,
  10–11
peacock, 62, 99–103, 146
peewit *see* lapwing
Pelecanus onocrotalus see
  pelican
pelican, 103–6
Pennsylvania, 98
Perigord, 26
Periphas, 42–3
Pershore Fair, 24
Persians, 45, 48, 62–3,
  103
Peter, St, 9–10, 151–2

petrel, storm, 32
Philippines, 96
Philomela, 83–4
Phineus, King, 39
Phoenicians, 36
Pica pica see magpie
Picus viridis see wood-
    pecker
pigeon, 66, 146
Pima Indians, 93
Pindar, 161–2, 165
Pliny the Elder, 9, 14,
    18, 27, 93, 98, 107–8,
    118, 141, 165
plover, 66
plumage
    black, 1–3, 116
    black and white, 79
    blue, 68
    red, 20, 21, 121–2,
    136, 139–40, 152–3
Plutarch, 137–8, 165
Plynlimmon, 45
Poland, 152–3
Portugal, 25, 136
Pragança, 25
Procne, 84
Prometheus, 43
proverbs, 96, 109
Prussia, 52
Psalms, 46
'puckeridge' 89–90
puffin, 56
Puruvaras, 142,
    144
pygmies, 15–18

Qin dynasty, 102
quail, 106–10

raven, 8, 32–3, 47, 66,
    79, 111–18, 140
'release' stone, 8,
    116–17
Remi, Bishop, 38
Revelations, 44
Rheims, 38
Rhodes, 134
robin, 66, 115, 118–24,
    159
Rolland, Eugene, 165
legend recorded by, 1–3
Romania, 151–2
Romans
    and cockerel/hen,
    6–7, 8, 9
    and crane, 18
    and cuckoo, 27
    and eagle, 43
    and goose, 50
    and owl, 93, 95, 97–8
    and quail, 107–8
    and raven, 113, 117–18
    and stork, 132
    and swan, 144
rook, 66, 125–8
Russia, 40, 45, 74, 109,
    135, 136, 137
Rutland, 126

sacred chickens, 6–7
sacredness, 32–4, 38
sacrifice, 7, 51, 154 *see
    also* wren hunt
St James's Day, 28
St John's Day, 28
St Martin's Day/Night,
    52, 72
St Vitus' Day, 116

salmonella, 107
Samoyedes, 144
sandpiper, green, 75
Saxicola torquata see
    stonechat
Scotland, 11, 25, 26, 28,
    30, 53, 80, 112, 121,
    128, 135, 154 *see also*
    Britain
Scots Magazine, The, 48
seagull, 32
Seb, 50, 57
Second World War, 113
Selborne, 89
Semiramis, 37
Serf, St, 121, 122
Seri, 103–4
Seychelles, 57
Shakespeare, William,
    165
    *The Comedy of
    Errors*, 75–6
    Hamlet, 76, 99
    Henry VI, Part III,
    46, 92–3
    Julius Caesar, 91–2
    King Lear, 71
    Love's Labours Lost,
    29
    Macbeth, 45, 95, 112
    Othello, 147
    The Rape of Lucrece,
    83
Shakir Padshah, Iman,
    38
Shang dynasty, 136
shearwater, 32
Sheba, Queen of, 40, 74
Shen ī king, 15–16

Shetland, 34, 48–9
Shropshire, 126
Shrove Tuesday, 7
Siberia, 13, 18, 30, 31–2, 34, 139, 144, 147
Sidney, Sir Philip, 41, 165
Sigurd, 114
Simorgh, 62–3
Singpho people, 10–11
Sioux Indians, 131
sleep, 87
snakes, 133, 160
Snowdon, Mount, 45
Snowdonia, 45
Solomon, King, 40, 63, 74–5, 86
Solway Firth, 53
Sonora, 103
souls of the dead, 32–3, 33–4, 75, 90, 93, 113, 126, 132, 137, 146
South America, 13
Southern Africa, 14, 136–7
sparrow *see* house sparrow
speech impediments, cure for, 141
spring, 22–4, 133–5
springwort, 60, 153–4
ṣṣāts, 48
Stedingers, 50
Stephen, St, 159
stonechat, 128–39
stones, 8, 14, 47–8, 108–9, 116–17, 140–1
stork, 8, 16, 33, 74, 130–3
Straits of Bosporus, 39

Streptopelia turtur see dove
Suffolk, 79, 119, 130
Sumeria, 41
Sussex, 79, 85
Swabia, 110
swallow, 8, 47, 66, 74, 84, 116, 121, 133–41, 159
swan, 66, 142–9
Swan, John, 165
Speculum mundi (The Mirror of the World), 98
Swan Lake, 142
Swazi, 136–7
Sweden, 51, 60, 73, 80, 95, 113, 151
Switzerland/the Swiss, 28, 110
Symplegades, 39
Syria/Syrians, 36, 37

Tam of Remeru, Jacob, 55
Tang dynasty, 102
Tara, 145
Tartars, 13, 70
Tchaikovsky, Piotr Ilyich: *Swan Lake*, 142
Tenbury fair, 24
Tengri, 139
Tereus, King of Thrace, 84
Teutonic Knights, 52
Theocritus, 29, 165
Second Idyll, 161
Thor, 118, 123, 149, 167

Thornax, Mount, 29
Thrace, 84
Thuringia, 19
Tiberius, Emperor, 117
Tibet, 113
Timandra, 90, 91
Titinius, 95, 165
Tlingit tribe, 115
tobacco, 13
Tochmarc Étaíne (The Wooing of Étaíne), 145–6
Topsell, Edward, 18, 165
Towednack cuckoo festival, 24
Tower of London, 113
Train, Joseph, 165
History of the Isle of Man, 158
Transylvania, 7
trees, 55–7
Trinidad, 13
Trinity Sunday, 157
Tristram, Sir, 29
Troglodytes troglodytes see wren
Troy/Trojan War, 67
Tsundige'wi, 16–17
Tulloch, Bobby, 48–9, 166
Tungus, 32
Turdus merula see blackbird
Turkestan, 38
Turkey, 96
Turner, Sir William, 54, 165
Tuscany, 110

Twelfth Night, 157
Tyrol, 60, 81, 110, 116, 119, 141
Tyto alba see owl

Unst, 49
Upupa epops see hoopoe
Urvasi, 142, 144

Valentinian, Emperor, 93
Vanellus vanellus see lapwing
Venezuela, 13
Veracruz, 17
Vikings, 114–15 *see also* Norse mythology
Villiers, 157
Vincent de Beauvais, 95, 166
Virgin Mary, 28, 37, 73, 121
vulture, 91

Wagner, Richard: *Lohengrin*, 142
Wales, 9, 27, 40, 45, 154 *see also* Britain
war/battles, 39–40, 44

warble fly, 90
Wayland Wood, 122
weather
    and blackbird, 3–4
    and cuckoo, 22, 23
    and diver, 34
    and eagle, 45
    and kingfisher, 70–1, 72
    and rook, 127
    and stonechat, 130
weathervanes, 10
Webster, John, 166
    The White Devil, 122–3
West Country, 11
Western Isles, 53
Westminster Abbey, 123
'Westminster Wonder, The', 123
Westphalia, 83, 135
White, Gilbert, 89–90, 166
Whitsun, 127
Whittier, John Greenleaf, 166
    'The Robin', 124
Wilde, Oscar: 'The Nightingale and the

Rose', 86
wishbone, 52
witchcraft, 95, 160
woodpecker, 59, 74, 99, 149–54
Wooing of Étaíne, The (Tochmarc Étaíne), 145–6
Worcestershire, 24
wren, 124, 146, 154–9
wren hunt, 154–7
wryneck, 60, 160–2
wyvern, 48

Yakuts, 30, 32
Yeats, William Butler, 166
    'The Cold Heaven', 126
Yenesei River, 30
Yorimoto, 39–40
Yorkshire, 25, 78, 90, 97, 127

Zeus, 29, 42–3, 83, 84, 91, 100–1, 144, 162, 167
Zulus, 136–7